Teaching Life

In this engaging book, Armand Doucet, a globally respected and recognized teacher, provides a clear roadmap for championing classroom-focused change in a technology-advanced society. *Teaching Life* brings the voices of teachers into the global conversation about educational reform to offer a how-to for implementing into classrooms design thinking, technology integration and a holistic education based on competencies, social-emotional learning and the literacies. With the innovative ideas in this book, educators can create a foundation for sustainable, honest, transparent leadership and work toward building a true community of local and global learning.

Armand Doucet is one of the world's foremost pracademics and teachers in education. He is a sought-after leader, inspirational speaker, coach, columnist and co-author of the best-selling book *Teaching in the Fourth Industrial Revolution: Standing at the Precipice* (Routledge 2018). Armand currently teaches Modern History and World Issues in French Immersion at Riverview High School in the Anglophone East School District in New Brunswick, Canada. He has received the Governor General Award for Teaching Excellence in History (2017), Canadian Prime Minister's Award for Teaching Excellence (2015), is a Meritorious Service Medal Recipient Governor General of Canada, an Apple Distinguished Educator, Teach SDGs Ambassador and has recently been nominated in the Top 50 for the Global Teacher Prize.

Routledge Leading Change Series

The world is crying out loud for quality education, and for the type of leadership and change to make quality education a reality. Never has there been a greater need for grasping the big pictures of leadership and change in education, which creates the world of tomorrow by developing future generations today.

In this series, you will find some of the world's leading intellectual authorities on educational leadership and change. From the pens of writers such as Dennis Shirley, Pak Tee Ng, Andy Hargreaves, Michael Fullan, Pasi Sahlberg, Alma Harris, Yong Zhao, Amanda Datnow, Vicky Park, Santiago Rincón-Gallardo, Armand Doucet and Karen Edge come wise insights and breakthrough ideas on this subject. They ask what the new imperatives of educational change are. They explore the paradoxical nature of educational change in celebrated Asian cultures and systems like those of Singapore. They point to the power of professional collaboration and leading from the middle in schools, networks of schools and across the world, rather than just driving change from the top. They invite us to think about and pursue educational change as social movements aimed at liberating learning. They highlight the surreal nature of leadership and change at this critical moment in world history.

This series of books is for the stout-hearted and open-minded reader who is keenly looking for inspiration to unlock the potential of educational leadership and change in this turbulent world.

Published Books in the Series Include

Teaching Life: Our Calling, Our Choices, Our Challenges
Armand Doucet

Professional Collaboration with Purpose: Teacher Learning Towards Equitable and Excellent Schools
Amanda Datnow and Vicki Park

For more information about this series, please visit: www.routledge.com/ Routledge-Leading-Change-Series/book-series/RLCS.

Teaching Life
Our Calling, Our Choices, Our Challenges

Armand Doucet

Routledge
Taylor & Francis Group

NEW YORK AND LONDON

First published 2019
by Routledge
52 Vanderbilt Avenue, New York, NY 10017

and by Routledge
2 Park Square, Milton Park, Abingdon, Oxon, OX14 4RN

Routledge is an imprint of the Taylor & Francis Group, an informa business

Library of Congress Cataloging-in-Publication Data
A catalog record for this book has been requested

ISBN: 978-1-138-37061-6 (hbk)
ISBN: 978-1-138-37063-0 (pbk)
ISBN: 978-0-429-42793-0 (ebk)

Typeset in Adobe Caslon Pro
by Apex CoVantage, LLC

Contents

Foreword

Sometimes wisdom comes from those who have arrived in our profession via circuitous paths. Armand's book is one of those unique perspectives that deepens our understanding of the current challenges facing our profession. Its strengths emanate from and are informed by the fact that he is a classroom teacher who joined our ranks after a career working with a wide array of actors in sales and nonprofits as well as mentoring students outside of school as a coach. His trajectory was launched by his creative attempts to reimagine school and the ways communities can engage in a process of redesign and student-centeredness. That experiment was so successful that he was nominated for the Global Teacher Prize, which connected him to a network of other innovative and committed educators from around the world. Among them, I am proud to say, is Education International's own teaching fellow, Jelmer Evers, who worked with the author on the co-creation of a teacher's response to education in the Fourth Industrial Revolution.

The strong ideas expressed in this book on teachers' learning and professional development (especially Chapters 2 and 3) make a compelling argument for a teaching and learning continuum. He rightly advocates a lifelong vision for teacher learning from initial teacher training throughout one's career and draws on international examples to make his case. In the tradition of Lee Schulman, he also advocates for purposeful mentoring and support for new teachers by more experienced ones in a hybrid Professional Development School's model of peer learning and reflection that sees career pathways from a professional teacher perspective and not from a profit-driven, managerialist one.

The book breaks new ground in the use of design thinking for classroom change and doubles down on Hargreaves's collaborative professionalism as the leading force for pedagogical experimentation and innovation. I especially found his case for how to systematically teach 'ideation' or brainstorming about collective ideas, iteration and feedback deeply powerful. He makes an important distinction between personalization for construction (in the context of each student's local culture, relationships and capacity) and personalization for instruction—the second of which could lead to top-down information-technology-led content delivery approaches currently in mode, with the big edu-businesses pitching machine learning instead of human learning.

For teacher union leaders, policymakers, school leaders and classroom teachers, this book is squarely focused on empowering the profession and giving teachers a professional voice in their schools and in the system. It effectively breaks down the current debates taking place within the profession about the future. Is it a 'managed occupation,' or is it a self-directed profession with a clear idea about the necessary conditions we must collectively ensure? The book is refreshing as it genuinely advances down a path of original thinking and reflection based on anecdotes drawn from Armand's own teaching. In a crowded field of 'how to' and 'how not to' books this book stands out. One the best, most original and unsentimental books I've read about teaching in ages.

David Edwards, Ph.D.
General Secretary, Education International

Acknowledgments

Writing a book is never a solo affair. Multiple people played a large role in bringing this one to life and the book would not exist without their passion, support and efforts.

My wife, Nicole, who never wavered in her support, understanding and patience during the writing of this book. As our house move literally and figuratively fell apart, while she was eight months pregnant and I am ready to get on a plane for Asia, she just looks at me and says, "We got this." Her rational thinking and calmness during the most trying times kept me focused as well as determined. This book doesn't exist without her passion for our family, for me, and her compassion as a wife and mother.

To my parents who took us in during the middle of the writing of this book for two months as we looked for a house. Having their house upheaval in the middle of their retirement must not have been easy, but like so many other times, they never flinched and made sure my daughters, wife and I felt welcomed and loved. No way I meet my deadlines without their uncanny ability to know when to help and the family support system they have developed and nurtured. My siblings, as they have always been: supportive, helpful, and babysat anytime I needed to stay late to brainstorm, do an interview, research or write.

To my co-editors, Andy Hargreaves and Pak Tee Ng, thank you for giving me this glorious opportunity to write in the Leading Change

Series with some of education's giants. The belief in me as a pracademic and that the voices of teachers should be heard I hope resonates throughout the book. Your feedback and mentorship were key in helping me filter my ideas and put them on paper.

Lisa Hrabluk, who has read every word in this book, deftly rewording and reorganizing multiple sections while instantly knowing how to make my voice stronger, I owe you a huge debt. Your remarkable care has made this book dramatically better by sharpening its argument, examples and style. Her standards are as high as can be and set the standard for what I tried to reach.

To my colleague and great friend Ian Fogarty, a true trailblazer in education, without your countless hours of indispensable support working side by side as I developed the ideas behind each chapter for this book, it doesn't see the light of day. You provided a sounding board enduring countless drafts, debates, designs and conversations to improve the substances and thoughtfulness. I will be forever grateful.

To the countless leaders that inspire me to be a professional every day I step into a classroom, give a keynote or write, you have given me the chance to explore the world of education and learn so much. In particular, Gregg Ingersoll, John McLaughlin, Chris Treadwell and all my principals, you have a gift that makes myself and my colleagues believe that we can be trailblazers in education even in our little part of the world.

To Andre Vincent and Rejean Boudreau of Assumption Life, as well as David Savoie of Acadian Construction, for your belief in education and the impact this book could have in propelling the discussion forward. Without your assistance, many of the observations, meetings and conferences, I would not have been able to attend. Social progress does not happen without dedication like yours in the belief that we can live in a better world.

Last but not least, to my colleagues, peers and friends in education all over the world and at home. The work that you do in the face of this disruptive age is genuinely amazing. I wake up every morning knowing that you are giving it your best every single minute of every single day and that I would dishonor you by not doing the same. Thank you for keeping me honest and hopeful that we will continue to push for the best education possible for our children.

Introduction

I found my path to teaching inside a prison on the other side of the world. Sitting in Nelson Mandela's jail cell on Robben Island will give anyone pause. It is small, uncomfortable and hauntingly lonely. After only a few minutes I began to feel claustrophobic and then angry that the South African government would keep him imprisoned in this small room for 30 years, taking him from his family and his freedom. Yet upon his release, Mandela did not react with vengeance as the system of apartheid crumbled and he and the African National Congress gained power. While some sought payback and punishment, Mandela saw a different future powered by reconciliation with the past and a strong effort to bridge understandings and realities in a highly polarized society. His tool was education.

Given the turbulent global landscape of today, Mandela's vision of education remains vital if we are to survive and flourish in our changing world. We are living in the Fourth Industrial Revolution, which is characterized by the fusing of physical, digital and biological systems.[1] Our world is changing at a rapid pace in this new digital age, profoundly impacted by automation and globalization. World Economic Forum founder and executive chairman Klaus Schwab states, "there has never been a time of greater promise, or greater peril."[2] Disruptive technologies and ecological changes are heralding widespread economic, social and political unrest, and communities are racing to figure out their place in our emerging new world. We see it everywhere. Teaching young people how to apply their knowledge and skills to solve the problems of our age has long been the promise—and expectation—of public education systems around the world and as change has accelerated, so too have demands to rethink education. The classroom many of us remember from our school days needs to change, but what is it changing into and how will those changes occur?

There's a global conversation happening about the future of education and teachers' voices need to be heard. Why? Because the change that is required can't happen without us. We are the practitioners and we bring to the conversation real-world experience that is necessary if the global community truly wants to formulate a new approach to education. Classroom teachers don't often get the chance to sit back and think about the big picture and our place within it. We're too busy teaching and dealing with our students who arrive every day in our classrooms with a multitude of perspectives, abilities and needs. Addressing students' immediate requirements while also delivering on curriculum goals is our priority, leaving us with little to no time to ponder the impact that technological, economic, social, political and environmental changes are having on our communities and the wider world. How do we teach something we ourselves do not fully understand? What are the major trends? What is the new innovation? How are current events affecting our classrooms?

American author, former venture capitalist and one of America's leaders in innovation, entrepreneurship and education, Ted Dintersmith chronicled some of this change in his books, including *What School Could Be: Insights and Inspiration from Teachers across America*. What he discovered as he crisscrossed the United States is many teachers and their students are doing extraordinary things in ordinary circumstances. "While a single spark is an anecdote, an aggregation suggests something more—a vision for the future of school, inspired by innovative teachers,"[3] he wrote.

Lucy Crehan, the author of the book *Cleverlands: The Secrets Behind the Success of the World's Education Superpowers*,[4] and a good friend, essentially took what she would describe as her "geeky gap year" away from teaching. With a gift for research, understanding and analysis, she spent two weeks each in Finland, Japan, Singapore, Shanghai and Canada, showcasing the education systems as well as the community support and culture. Her book inspired me to take a closer look at the stories behind the data, as my experience is that teachers are trying in many parts of the world such as Ted describes for the United States.

This new vision is about more than simply preparing students for a more technologically advanced world. It is about preparing them to critically think about the world we want to live in and how to accomplish that goal, to be able to identify and then navigate their way through the promise and peril that Schwab and others foretold. This requires a holistic approach to learning that includes ethical, civil, social, economic, ecological and technological considerations. How else to prepare our students for a world where gene editing, weaponized social networks and mass economic automation are commonplace? How will they redefine civil society in a world in which physical, biological and digital systems mix and merge? What will they value? How will they seek common ground with others, be they across the street or around the globe? How will universal human rights such as equity, justice, peace and freedom be reflected in the Fourth Industrial Revolution?

It is the job of the education system to prepare students to answer these fundamental questions, which means the bulk of the responsibility lies with teachers. Change usually enters our classrooms via our students, who are quick to adopt and use new technologies, frequently without thinking too deeply about the repercussions. That task falls to teachers, who are often the first to see the impacts of technology, particularly mental health issues such as depression, anxiety and isolation that mobile technologies and social media have wrought. At the same time, many teachers seek to embrace this new world, integrating changes into our lesson plans. It is in the details of the designed learning experiences for all students that teachers reflect and understand the gravity of the situation and the need for an ethical response as well as to showcase leadership and benefits for our communities in this digital age. Technology can enhance learning but teacher must use these new tools thoughtfully and with care, otherwise it can have a detrimental effect in our classrooms and with our students. Don't assume just because a school is 'teched out' that it is also pedagogically advanced.

As an example, at one school I visited, educators were initially excited to introduce cloud-based peer editing—until they discovered students were simply clicking 'select all' to accept all changes, which resulted in a better document but not in better writers. In this digital age, the nuances shown in this example perfectly support our need for continued, calculated, personalized and professional growth for each teacher. Teaching is a profession populated by the naturally curious, and we must support this curiosity with specialized training and postgraduate degrees to be the best teachers possible for the nuances of today's education.

A Teacher's Voice

Over the past decade I have had the good fortune to meet and work with teachers who understand the challenges and are already working at changing the education system from within. It is not an easy task. They face argumentative parents, dogmatic politicians, risk-averse administrators, indifferent colleagues and, let's be honest, classrooms of varying sizes with a mixture of students, some of whom love to learn while others would love to be anywhere else. It can make for trying days. But we also know parents who seek to be our partners in the education of their children; we have benefited from the support of administrators who create environments for professional growth and creativity; we gravitate toward colleagues who are equally enthused for our shared calling; and we are inspired by the enthusiasm of our students. To be teachers at this point in history is to live and work in interesting times.

When Andy asked if I would contribute to this series as a teacher in the classroom, I was taken aback, nervous and overwhelmed. It is a daunting task to put forward a global perspective of the teaching profession in this time of change, and it is a responsibility I do not take lightly. Who am I to tell this story? I am a high school history teacher in a small city on the East Coast of Canada. I have been teaching for a decade, finding my passion after a career in sales and marketing, an experience that taught me the value of person-to-person networks. I've also been coaching amateur athletes since I was a teenager.

In late 2013 a parent nominated me for a new international award, the Varkey Foundation's $1 million Global Teacher Prize. While I didn't make the short list, I was curious. The prize was to be awarded in March 2014 in Dubai as part of the Global Skills and Education Forum, the Varkey Foundation's annual conference, and the speaker list was a who's who of world leaders. I tapped into both my family's and my own business networks and was able to raise enough money for the plane ticket and an inexpensive (for Dubai) hotel room for a few days. At the forum, I met and spoke with government officials, wealthy philanthropists and people from international NGOs (non-governmental organizations) interested in systems change. It was quite a rush, and I decided I wanted to be a part of this global conversation.

I have returned to the Global Education and Skills Forum each year since, and I was honored to be named to the Global Teacher Prize's Top 50 in 2017, which brought me into a global community of amazing educators working to transform their classrooms and schools for the 21st century. That experience inspired me and five of my colleagues—Jelmer Evers (the Netherlands), Elisa Guerra (Mexico), Nadia Lopez (New York, USA), Michael Soskil (Pennsylvania, USA) and Koen Timmers (Belgium)—to co-author *Teaching in the Fourth Industrial Revolution: Standing at the Precipice*, a reflection of the conversations we were having with our peers.

My pre-teaching experiences in sales and coaching meant I was never going to be the 'sage on the stage' kind of teacher. I like riffing off of other people's ideas and encouraging those around me to combine their personal passions with hard work to achieve big goals. In my first few years I was young, fearless and somewhat naïve. I thought I was a great teacher, making a major difference in my student's lives, just like those heroic teachers portrayed in the movies I love. Very early in my teaching career I began designing classroom plans that allowed me to use students' personal interests to teach them the curriculum. For instance, one year I conceived and then managed a school-wide project that uses the world of Harry Potter to teach kids math, literacy, science, social studies, art and music. We converted the middle school into Hogwarts, a feat that caught the attention of media worldwide. It was lots of fun and it got our students excited about learning, but it was completely unsustainable. It required too many additional resources—volunteer time from parents, extra working hours from teachers and financial support from the local business community—to be replicated year after year. My local system simply was not equipped to enable this kind of classroom-centered innovation, a problem that is endemic across education.

While it was a great project and we pulled off a few more major cross-disciplinary school-wide learning experiences, it taught me the power of trusting each other as professional teachers. Collaboration with your peers and colleagues when genuine and moving toward the same goal is some of the best professional development I have had in my career. Through working on these projects, my colleagues taught me how to build relationships with disenfranchised students, how school setting and the right culture can inspire students to greater heights, the power of social media to enhance the learning of students, the importance of developing social-emotional learning and how to plan together for success of all students. No one was left behind.

Ours was a successful grassroots initiative, with the right teachers, good chemistry and great community partnerships. Many grassroots success stories in education have this similar formula. The best intentions of policymakers to replicate success on a larger scale result in mass policies that negate the importance of the ingredients in the formula. A classic example of this is when professional learning communities were the rage in North America: Some teams worked great and some didn't. The authenticity, the need, the desire, the processes, the time, the structures all play a part. Professor Linda Darling-Hammond, founder of Stanford Center for Opportunity and Policy in Education, whose long list of accolades and positions is only surpassed by her influence on education in the United States, wrote:

> Bureaucratic solutions to problems of practice will always fail because effective teaching is not routine, students are not passive, and questions of practice are not simple, predictable, or standardized. Consequently, instructional decisions cannot be formulated on high, then packaged and handed down to teachers.[5]

The past decade has been peppered with new education models, pedagogies, policies and assessments—all emanating from the top without much regard for how they will impact teachers in the classroom. Often these changes are introduced with little to no engagement with individual teachers, who are frustrated at the lack of consensus on how to progress from policymakers and politicians. This is what we talk about in our staff rooms. We do not want to read another study or attend another policy seminar that speaks of change as something that awaits us somewhere in the future or which will be delivered by a distant government directive. We are no longer content to make incremental adjustments that leave the backbone of the system untouched. We are impatient with procrastination, lamenting that the day is fast approaching when superficial efforts will be insufficient to maintain pace with the needs of society. This is what I and my colleagues around the world experience in our classrooms: well-intentioned policy and curriculum changes driven from the top with no rationalization or explanation for our classrooms.

A Lesson Plan for Change

I am selfish. I have a passion for education, and so I have set out on a quest to understand what is happening in the world and in education so that I can be a better teacher for my students. But, this has been hard on my friends and family as I push to understand. It has been an eye-opening, exciting, scary, energetic and exhausting personal journey. What I have learned gives me hope. To begin, we have a strong foundation in public education upon which to build. We must strengthen and enhance our public systems to meet the needs of all children regardless of gender, race, creed, location or economic standing. Second, there is growing recognition of the urgency for educational change among teachers, union leaders, policymakers, parents, academics, politicians, philanthropists, nonprofit leaders and businesspeople.

This is a book for and about teachers. It is also a book for anyone interested in championing classroom-focused change. The task is not without its challenges. Current debates about education are rife with polarizing opinions on a variety of topics including professional training, technology in the classroom, content, pedagogy, metrics and assessment. There are many strongly held beliefs about education, with intense emotional ties. Teachers' words and behaviors, particularly those trying to bring change to their classrooms, are being judged by others—parents, peers, administrators, community members, politicians and businesspeople— all of whom view the system through the lens of their experiences as students decades earlier. Everyone has an opinion about what's wrong with education, and they freely share it with teachers.

In response, teachers are increasingly opting to align with various theories and processes, such as STEM or STEAM, Advanced Placement or International Baccalaureate, project-based or college-ready learning. The label is irrelevant; it's about good teaching practice, which really involves all these labels. However, instead of looking at how these labels combine for great practice, we have witnessed a polarization of the teaching profession; new vs. old, behaviorism vs. constructivism, teacher-centered vs. student-centered, Pavlov vs. Piaget vs. Dewey. Clutching strongly to a particular label and dogma does not contribute to healthy dynamics for school-centered change.

Because education is so critical and a personal journey for each individual, there is often significant and deep running emotion attached to individual points of view. It becomes about the personal rather than the greater good, which leads to opinion-driven rather than fact-driven decision-making. A clarification is due for what it means to make decisions based on fact-driven decision-making. It should embrace a values-driven, ethical decision-making model that takes into account the big/small data as well as stories that surround the front lines of education in our classroom. One must be careful what we consider a fact. Faces and stories contribute to big data.

Digital technology has played its role in this polarization, bringing out the good and bad in our society. While it has enabled us to connect with more people, it has also fed our fears. The public square has given way to walled gardens of like-minded people, the exact opposite of what we need to solve the problems of our age. Healthy debate in service to creative problem-solving has been stifled, resulting in noisy, nasty rhetoric across and within countries. Instead of bringing us together to solve problems, this digital age's potential has been squandered on widening an inequity gap to the breaking point of our humanity and world.

We need to refine and rediscover our common humanity. I have been lucky enough over the last few years to be part of various global teacher networks, which has given me the opportunity to grow and to speak with researchers, business leaders, politicians and community leaders who are invested in finding a way forward. It has enabled me to reflect on the meaning of education. I purposefully consider the foundations of each strategy, program and philosophy, often playing devil's advocate to test the validity of each.

In the last five years I have keynoted, facilitated and participated in professional development around the globe. My thirst for learning always propelled me to stay a few more days to collaborate with colleagues, see classrooms, meet students, talk with education experts in multiple countries and discover the intricacies of educating in different cultures. A network of colleagues, an abundance of great pedagogical practices and an understanding of differences between many education jurisdictions have been some of the benefits. I have witnessed the great, the bad and the ugly. Transoceanic flights on long weekends to attend one- or two-day conferences gave me a new understanding for the word 'jet-lagged.' Having leadership and administration that believed in the power of collaboration, innovation and learning by networking gave me the flexibility to be outside the classroom as they saw direct benefits for my students. That type of leadership is not the norm for many teachers around the world, and I find this deeply troubling. My experiences should not be the exception; they should be the norm. I firmly believe that teachers can and should spearhead change in our education systems, but they cannot do this working in isolation. They must be encouraged and trained in how to share, collaborate, lead and communicate as master teachers networking with others in order to scale best practices and models in their classrooms, schools and districts.

This book examines how to do that in service to driving global change, from the classroom up.

How This Book Is Organized

I've divided the book into two sections.

Part I, "Our Calling," considers how teachers' own attitudes toward the profession have changed, how society is influencing this evolution and how teachers should proceed in pursuit of being lifelong learners, including a call to action to embrace teaching as an action-oriented profession, with accompanying roles and responsibilities, and the rejection of teaching as a passive occupation.

Part II, "Our Choices and Our Challenges," shares my learnings, gained from my professional practice and interviews with innovative teachers around the world, showcasing the "how" of classroom change. This section also examines the complex issues confronting teachers in this era of massive technological and political change and offers a blueprint for welcoming change into the classroom.

Teachers know we don't have the luxury of time when it comes to educational change. Every morning when we walk into our classrooms, change is waiting for us. Our students are there, waiting. Waiting to be inspired. Waiting for their needs to be met. Waiting to learn. Waiting to be led. That is the challenge and the promise that greets every teacher, every day.

It is why teachers need to be active participants in the design of education's new path. We are the professionals in the field with the expertise and the tools to help figure it out. We know it will take a holistic view to reach the broader goals of education in the Fourth Industrial Revolution, which includes the development of social-emotional learning as well as new competencies and new skills. Teachers understand and can articulate the obstacles in trying to implement this vision and what is needed to fully realize this plan.

I have reason for hope. Teachers around the world are leading the charge in finding new ways to reach each and every child. This book tells their stories.

Notes

1. Doucet, Armand, Evers, Jelmer, Guerra, Elisa, Lopez, Nadia, Soskil, Michael, and Timmers, Koen (2018) *Teaching in the Fourth Industrial Revolution: Standing at the Precipice.* Abingdon: Routledge.
2. Hutt, Rosamund (2016, January 23) "9 Quotes That Sum Up the Fourth Industrial Revolution." *World Economic Forum.* www.weforum.org/agenda/2016/01/9-quotes-that-sum-up-the-fourth-industrial-revolution/
3. Dintersmith, Ted (2018) *What School Could Be: Insights and Inspirations from Teachers across America.* Princeton: Princeton University Press.
4. Crehan, Lucy (2017) *Cleverlands: The Secrets Behind the Success of the World's Education Superpowers.* London: Unbound.
5. Darling-Hammond, Linda (1997) *The Right to Learn: A Blueprint for Creating Schools That Work.* San Francisco: Jossey-Bass.

PART I
OUR CALLING

1

TEACHERS STAND ALONE

My first teaching job was a long-term supply placement that began in January, halfway through the school year. I thought I had arrived well-prepared. Months earlier, I met with the teacher I was replacing: an experienced, well-organized professional who happily shared her teaching plans with me and offered advice on teaching methods and the school's culture. I had the support of the principal and vice principal. However, nothing prepared me for the level of exhaustion I felt at the end of my first day of teaching.

Walking in on that first day, I thought 'okay, I've got this.' And then reality set in. I was teaching eight different subjects—grades 6, 7 and 8 science, grades 6 and 7 social studies and grade 6 math and French. I had a degree in kinesiology and a bachelor's degree in education, with which I can teach elementary and secondary school, but math and French were not my specialties. Yes, I was raised in a bilingual family and I obviously needed math to study kinesiology, but knowing a subject and knowing how to teach a subject are two different skills. Nonetheless, I did what all new teachers do: I plunged in, staying up late into the night to review my lesson plans for the next day and following my predecessor's detailed notes.

I came home that first night exhausted, and as the week progressed my exhaustion grew. Teaching class after class of 11-, 12- and 13-year-olds is emotionally draining. At this age students require a mix of foundational blocks of learning, the tail end of their elementary education, and higher critical thinking and creative learning, the precursor to what awaits them in high (secondary) school. Throw in the hormonal, physical and emotional changes of puberty and you have the crazy, exhilarating mix that is middle school. A typical day could mean teachers must balance explaining basic algebra alongside the drama of first dates and the inevitable first breakups, or English literature amid student anxiety and feelings of low self-esteem. Teachers around the world face this every day, and they do so in isolation.

This is a defining feature of our current education culture: Teachers stand alone. Certainly, that has been the model that successive education systems have followed for centuries. The singular sage on the stage: a well-respected, educated individual standing at the front of the classroom, lecturing their students who sit quietly in neat rows of desks, passively listening and learning. It is a model adapted from the previous industrial revolution and instituted in our schools. Even though this has been the dominant model, there have been previous attempts to introduce alternate teaching models. For instance, the progressive teaching movement in England of the 1960s and '70s had varying degrees of success. However, it was denigrated by the global managerial reform movement in education, which emphasized checks and balances. But while the teaching profession struggled to change with the times, outside education other industries were evolving, introducing more collaborative and fluid workplace models. It is with a sad irony that I note teachers are increasingly encouraged to teach collaborative decision-making and team building to prepare students for the world of work in the 21st century while their own work environment remains wedded to the past.

Prior to becoming a teacher, I worked a decade in sales and marketing for a multinational food and beverage company. Within a couple of weeks of being hired in New Brunswick, I was flown halfway across the country to the company's Canadian headquarters in Toronto for a week of team building and corporate training. Alongside other new recruits, we learned the ins and outs of the company, its expectations of us and how to support each other as we adjusted to our new roles. I left that week feeling confident in both my role within the company but also in the network of support available to me. My personal success was the company's success. I was part of a team.

Juxtapose that with my teaching career. Every day I walk into my classroom and I am off and running. The old image of teachers hanging out in the staff room is an outdated stereotype that doesn't reflect the reality of today's teaching profession. We enter our classrooms ahead of our students and the official start of the school day, which usually starts around 8:20 a.m. We are there through each period in the morning, with only a couple of minutes between classes that is usually occupied by students lingering to chat or for extra help. Over lunch we provide extra help or run a school club. After wolfing down a quick lunch, we are back in front of our whiteboards or smart boards, teaching the next subject with little prep time between classes. After the final bell rings, we might be volunteering with another school club, talking with parents about a struggling student or settling in to mark student work, documenting their learning through detailed charts, forms and computer software designed to measure and analyze student achievement. The typical school day leaves teachers with no time to collaborate with our peers, to bounce ideas off each other or to seek support and guidance. What's the best practice for interacting with parents? What relationship should I expect and receive from administrators? How can I integrate design learning into the curriculum? How do I support my peers and how do they support me? Questions that in another profession would be answered in the first week are left unasked and unanswered by most new teachers.

Collaboration with peers, the ability to interact with experts and time for self-reflection on practice, pedagogy and students are all vital to answer complex questions involving the interplay between forces outside your classroom, or outside the school, which may be in conflict with each other; the politics of school committees; local politics and its influence on education; the impact of political shifts on education programs and the classroom; topics such as language of instruction; religion in schools; sex education; educating refugees and immigrants; and education for work vs. education for self-actualization. These are complex questions and no one teacher can answer them. Collaborating with peers and experts and being given the time for self-reflection can help in trying to find answers and solutions that are appropriate for each teacher's context.

Teachers, as the old saying goes, "aren't here for the money." Becoming a teacher is more than a career choice; it is for many of us a calling. Take for instance Estella Afi Owoimaha-Church of California. She says her parents' belief in education made her want to enter the profession. The daughter of immigrants, Estella is the eldest of three children and the first in her family to graduate college. There was always a lot of pressure on her to do well in school to repay the debt to the country. And on top of that, she was taught that moving through the world in service of others was the way to go. An example of that was her dad helping them pack their lunches for school and packing extra lunches either for kids at school who needed them or for any homeless person they might pass on the way to school. For Estella, teaching was the best way to serve and give back to her community.

On the other side of the world in Vietnam, Nam Thanh Ngo knows what it's like to grow up in poverty and the sacrifices his family made to pay for his education, including paying for textbooks, uniforms and school fees. When choices must be made to spend money on food or school, education doesn't usually win. Yet Nam's parents still sent him to school. In grade 5 his curiosity was awakened by Ms. Hoa, who used creative lessons and experiments to coax Nam to excel at school. Her efforts continue to inspire Nam, who decided to become a teacher to spark other children's love of learning in the same way Ms. Hoa sparked his, and in doing so, helped him lift himself and his family out of poverty.

For me, it was the day my mom took me to see my first film in a movie theatre. It was *E.T. The Extra-Terrestrial*, and I can remember it as if it was yesterday: the red carpet going into the cinema; the smell of popcorn and the excitement of settling into those big comfy seats as the lights dimmed. I was mesmerized by the story. I smiled over the Reese's Pieces, bounced excitedly in my seat when Elliott freed the frogs and I cried—really cried—when the adults watched impassively as E.T. lay dying. It was gut-wrenching. On the walk home, I asked my mom why the adults wouldn't help E.T. and she said something that has stayed with me.

> What is someone's perception may not be the same for another. You need to try and understand each other to build bridges to understand and live together. Not everyone wants to build consensus. When someone only wants to be right, that's when the world has problems.

Right then and there, I knew I wanted to be one of the people that helped build bridges for the greater good. It's why I love coaching and it is why I finally made my way to teaching. Being a teacher allows me to stay true to the promise I made to myself all those years ago.

However, as with many professions, the reality of today's educator workplace doesn't live up to the dream.

You want to be innovative, but the standardized test gets in the way.

You want to be around the content, but you're teaching a subject you flunked in high school.

You want to individualize and inspire, but you are not allowed to differ from the mandated lesson plan.

You would like to spend time doing extra help, but you have paperwork to do.

You want to work and build community, but there's no time to work with fellow teachers or outside resources.

You would like to do technology integration, but half the class can't afford technology.

You would like to spend some time with your family, but you have marking and planning to do.

You would like to do extracurricular activities, but your spouse gets mad at how much time you spend away from your family.

This is why teachers leave.

They are broken because they realize wanting to make a difference in their students' lives isn't valued as much as it once was.

They lose hope because administrators and bureaucrats dissuade them from doing something different or creative in their classrooms.

They become discouraged because they feel powerless in the face of politically motivated curriculum and funding changes.

They are disheartened by the 'teach to the test' demands of high-stakes testing and assessments that drive funding.

The joint general secretary of the National Education Union in England, Kevin Courtney, in a 2018 *Guardian* article states that "81 per cent of teachers have considered leaving the profession in the last year because of workload, driven in large part by time-consuming data gathering that has little or nothing to do with children's education."[1] Another article in the *Guardian* by Sarah Marsh (2015) cited that

> [Seventy-three] per cent of trainee teachers had thought to leave the profession. . . . More than 54 per cent said they did not think they'd be teaching in 10 years' time . . . 76 per cent cited the heavy workload as the major reason . . . 53 per cent state they have insufficient time to reflect on their practice. . . . In France, a meagre 5 per cent of teachers feel valued.[2]

Is it any wonder that the world faces a shortage of 69 million teachers by 2030?[3]

According to the US National Education Association (NEA), there is a direct correlation between teachers' economic positions over the last 20 years and the way they are recognized/valued in comparison to other professions with a similar amount of schooling. "Teachers earn 19 per cent less than similarly skilled and educated professionals today. This 'teaching penalty' has increased significantly in the past 20 years—from approximately 2 per cent in 1994 to 19 per cent in 2017."[4]

In some regions, most notably some areas of the United States, teacher compensation is tied to high-stakes testing and assessment. For instance, the development of the OECD's (Organisation for Economic Co-operation and Development) Programme for International Student Assessment (PISA) in the early 2000s occurred just as politicians and policymakers were considering how to measure education results. PISA has famously become a way for countries and regions to compare their education system against the rest of the world. Now, I am not saying that we should not have standardized testing. I do believe that it does give you an idea of where you stand. But it should not be the driving force in long-term policy decisions, nor should it be used to reinforce top-down decision-making to drive more structure, accountability measures and strict guidelines.

In fact, PISA's results point to the value of that statement. Finland and Singapore, which have consistently been PISA leaders, subscribe to a view of teaching that supports and encourages teacher professionalism and creativity in the classroom. Pak Tee Ng has written the definitive book on Singapore's education system. Singapore's uniqueness has given him the opportunity, as the associate dean of leadership learning at the National Institute of Education (NIE), to mentor all the principals and teachers in the city-state. He states that

> quality will be driven by teachers and leaders in the schools, with ideas bubbling up through the system, rather than be pushed down from the top . . . they are in the best position to develop new approaches to engage their students.[5]

Change needs to happen from the bottom up, but also the top down.

Standardized testing used poorly leads to bad policy that forces teachers to 'teach to the test' and further reinforces their disillusionment. Just recently, New York State removed the mandatory use of standardized testing results as part of the teacher and administrator evaluation process. Teachers want to reach kids. Unfortunately, high-stakes testing can be disastrous for the teaching profession and (by extension) students if the results are not properly interpreted, recognizing the culture, values, social structures, health and economic ability of each region. Each can have a profound effect on student learning but are hardly ever mentioned when politicians start to talk about education. The world is constantly asking for educators to be trailblazers: to develop competencies, social-emotional learning, skills and curriculums while really concentrating most policy decisions on reform on standardized testing of curriculum content allocating resources toward this metric. It's a paradox that isn't lost on the classroom teachers who are facing pressures to be more professional, action-based researchers finding a way to manage all these pillars, while getting at the same time the real pressure of only needing one metric to survive: scores on a test. This needs to change for education to flourish for all. It is the dilemma that keeps me up at night. It is the dilemma that I see ripping education apart. It is the dilemma that is killing the teaching profession in many areas around the world.

Diane Ravitch, research professor of education at New York University, is considered one of the eminent writers and researchers on the American education system. In her blog, she states:

> when the measure becomes the goal, and when people are punished or rewarded for meeting or not meeting the goal, the measure is corrupted. . . .

Do not attach high stakes to evaluations, or both the measure and the outcome will become fraudulent.[6]

In our race to tell the big data story of a country's relative success in education, we are omitting and devaluing the small data stories in individual classrooms. This is where change takes hold in education. Why? Because the story of education is the story of individual successes.

There is hope. Teachers are standing up for their rights as professionals, and what feels different is that teachers are actively fighting for a new path in education. Self-reflection on the purpose of education and the purpose of teaching is not being driven anymore from agendas outside of our school walls but from within the teaching profession itself. In 2018, teachers in West Virginia, Oklahoma and Arizona fought for support staff, appropriate classroom sizes and adequate school budgets to achieve educational outcomes. And teachers are not alone in their fight. Parents, nonprofits and businesses want to help local schools and teachers. "Teachers are turning this moment into a movement," said American Federation of Teachers (AFT) president Randi Weingarten. She continued: "The walkouts not only secured immediate gains for kids' learning and teacher pay, they were a catalyst for educators to run for office to fix the state and local governments that failed them."[7]

This catalyst for rallying together for the greater good of education is seeing teachers take ownership of the profession and realizing that education is only going to improve if we the teachers are willing to change. We know that we need to develop competencies with more intent. We know we are going to have to do more social-emotional learning from K-12, getting our students ready to be resilient, adaptable and capable of managing their anxieties and worries as they face an uncertain future. We know we need to personalize education to help all learners reach their full potential. We know we need to protect our students from data collectors and arm them to navigate in this new age with the ability to understand who is trying to influence them. We know we need to integrate new technology to help them flourish in this digital age, but we also know that not all new technology is good. We know that knowledge and curriculum content scaffolding is still important; it is a myth that you can just google everything and get the answers you seek. Comparisons, correlations and cross-thinking take a certain amount of content knowledge to be able to grow and innovate, building on ideas from other sectors and within each individual subject. For example, certain math knowledge and skills are the foundation to do complex architecture, coding, computational thinking, physics and medicine.

To build this complex education system, we are going to need help from all sectors in order to move forward, and we will have to let go of some parts of our practice. As Bradley Cooper's character sings in the movie *A Star is Born*, "maybe it's time to let the old ways die." Teachers need to step up into leadership to help define and design new learning pathways, but they must make space for others to co-create a student-centric system. All of us—teachers, parents, administrators, politicians, policymakers and businesspeople—must let the old ways die and embrace a new way of learning and teaching. We must let go of our long-held perspectives on education—most likely formed from our own experiences as students decades earlier or our understanding of what may or may not be happening in our children's schools. This perception of what is happening in our classrooms versus the reality seems to me (as a teacher) to be one of the major issues affecting the ability of schools to become truly effective.

For education systems, the easiest path is the one of least resistance and the one that can be evaluated the quickest. So when we want to cut down, we use assessment data that represents what a child knows of content from a certain subject. It can also include some competencies depending on the subject, but the assessment needs to be designed so that it is simple to grade. The perception is that it is simple. The truth is quite different. The easy path in education has been taken many times and it has never produced excellence. Take professional development: Standards have dropped in many systems around the world. Programs promise to develop teachers in only six weeks after they graduate from university; this is a promise that doesn't come close to the reality. And yet politicians and policymakers embrace these for-profit companies that develop professional development programs or initial teacher education programs outside of the school systems because they promise to improve education's bottom line. That's putting the system ahead of students—the equivalent of putting the store ahead of the customer.

In many education systems around the world, our calling to teach is not aligned with the realities of being a teacher in highly bureaucratic, metrics-heavy, financially strapped school systems. Leaders in these systems are managers, checking off boxes. No one wants to take responsibility for defining the purpose of education and then designing a system that lives up to those ideals.

It is time to revisit why people go into the profession, what makes them stay and how we can grow the next generation of educators to lead our profession forward.

Notes

1. Weale, Sally (2018, October 4) "Teacher Crisis Hits London as Nearly Half Quit within Five Years." *Guardian*. www.theguardian.com/education/2018/oct/04/teacher-crisis-hits-london-as-nearly-half-quit-within-five-years
2. Marsh, Sarah (2015, January 27) "Five Top Reasons People Become Teachers – and Why They Quit." *Guardian*. www.theguardian.com/teacher-network/2015/jan/27/five-top-reasons-teachers-join-and-quit
3. UNESCO (2016, October 5) "Close to 69 Million New Teachers Needed to Reach 2030 Education Goals." http://www.unesco.org/new/en/media-services/single-view/news/close_to_69_million_new_teachers_needed_to_reach_2030_educat/
4. National Education Association (2018, September) "Teacher Compensation: Fact vs. Fiction." www.nea.org/home/12661.htm
5. Ng, Pak Tee (2017) *Learning from Singapore: The Power of Paradoxes*. New York: Routledge.
6. Ravitch, Diane (2017, December 27) "Settling for Scores: Why Are Schools Still Judged by the Results of Standardized Tests?" *New Republic*. https://newrepublic.com/article/145935/settling-scores
7. Elk, Mike (2018, September 7) "The Fight Continues: Which States Will Teachers Strike in Next?" *Guardian*. www.theguardian.com/us-news/2018/sep/07/teachers-strike-next-walkout-when-will-it-be-dates

2

PROFESSION OR
OCCUPATION?

Stop me if you've heard this one before. A teacher decides to do something special for their class. They redesign a unit of the prescribed curriculum and inject it with pop culture references their students love. They reach out into the wider community for donations of supplies, stay up late and dedicate their weekends to planning out this unit. The new unit is a hit with students, who proudly show off what they've accomplished to their parents, some of whom reach out to congratulate the teacher and thank them for their efforts. A few days later, still basking in the success of the unit, the teacher receives a note to visit the office after school. Thinking they are being called in to talk about how to keep the momentum going, they soon realize that's not what's going on. Instead, they're told that while the administration is impressed with their efforts—really, they are—some "people" don't think it's appropriate. Or maybe someone in the district or departmental office doesn't like all this attention being placed on a single class. It doesn't matter the reason—the heart of the message is always the same: Don't try that again. Stick to the department-approved program.

I remember the first time I got called in to an administrator's office. I thought I was going to have an experience like the one above, based on a number of friends and colleagues in jurisdictions around the world who have made similar trips to similar offices. That wasn't my experience. I was treated like a professional. The leadership supported the methods I utilized to try and reach kids where they were and get them excited about learning. In truth, my experience has been one of professional collaboration with my administrators and leaders. They have led me through this digital age with a common question between them: "How does it help student learning?" Their pursuit to answer this simple yet complex question has pushed them to evolve the leadership model of administration that is trying to control every second of every moment of learning in every classroom of their schools. They seek positive progression to reach every student. It is inspiring and empowering when your leaders trust you. From them I have learned what it means to delegate, trust and engage your workforce to showcase their strengths versus trying to micro-manage their weaknesses.

A conundrum in education is created when teachers are told they are members of a profession but then are treated as workers in an occupation. Defining who and what we want to be will require teachers, administrators, policymakers, politicians and parents to confront long-simmering issues of control, leadership and self-identity. To be blunt, we need to practice what we teach.

There is a growing consensus around the world that classrooms must evolve to prepare students for the 21st century by teaching global competencies—the core foundation required to live and work in a knowledge-based society. These include critical thinking and problem-solving; innovation, creativity and entrepreneurship; self-awareness and self-direction; collaboration; communications; and global citizenship and sustainability. But how can we teach these competencies to anyone if we aren't developing these competencies within ourselves and the systems in which we work? As Sir Ken Robinson once said, "If you design a system to do something, don't be surprised if it does it."[1] It is the difference between being directed in how and what to teach by others as opposed to co-creating a dynamic learning environment with partners, peers and supportive system leaders.

I liken it to the difference between famous chefs and media personalities Gordon Ramsey and the late Anthony Bourdain. Both are successful and admired, but very different in their approach to food. There's no mistaking what Gordon Ramsay considers the elements of a good restaurant. On his various TV shows, he demands strict adherence to his model. That's how to run a busy commercial kitchen: by reproducing signature dishes of quality night after night. There's one creative master—the head chef—and everyone else's job is to recreate the chef's vision. That's akin to the expectations of teachers working within the occupation model: Follow the curriculum, don't deviate and repeat. This was fine for content-based education only. Memorize, test and repeat through the system, which was appropriate for the masses of the 19th and 20th centuries in gaining basic skills. Yet it was already being challenged from the 1960s onward, knowing that future students would need more.

Anthony Bourdain started out in that system, and as head chef of Les Halles in New York City, he would have likely run his kitchen in much the same way. Why? Because it is a proven model that works. But then he stepped off that path and decided to explore the underlying culture of food, from harvest to table and everything in between. With his award-winning series, *Parts Unknown*, Bourdain brought us into his journey, creating a learning experience that showcased the common elements of our cultures and explored the human condition in a way that invited us to evaluate our beliefs and values. As President Barack Obama posted on Twitter following Bourdain's death in 2018: "He taught us about food—but more importantly, about its ability to bring us together. To make us a little less afraid of the unknown."[2] As Bourdain learned, we learned too, and we connected with him not because he presented himself as the all-knowing expert but because he welcomed us in with a mix of humility and curiosity. His fallibility was his strength.

This way of teaching by collaborating with all walks of life, including colleagues and peers, is the definition of professional for me. It's about being a lifelong learner with the ability to make decisions when issues arise based on your experience, what's best for the profession and the people affected by it. It's about the people around you trusting that you will be able to do it. It's about you trusting yourself that you have the knowledge and tools to do the job at hand. This differs greatly from an occupation. We as teachers need to follow Bourdain's lead and step outside the prescribed high-stakes testing model of classroom teaching, which varies around the world, and head off with an open heart and a curious mind to parts unknown. Why? Because just as we teach our students that they will someday likely work in jobs we can't imagine today, logically we as teachers will need to be equally adaptable in how we teach. Do we want to be professionals who have the content, pedagogical expertise and training to create a personalized setting for each child based on their strengths and weaknesses while recognizing the values and beliefs of the community? Or would we prefer a standardized, easily accountable, easily scalable, check-the-boxes type of system that does not recognize the uniqueness of our communities and students, where everybody is fed exactly the same thing at the same time, on the same day? Is that education? No, for me it is not.

Globally, it has quickly become apparent to me that the debate over the role of teachers—a managed occupation versus a self-directed profession—will be a deciding factor in whether an education system fails, maintains the status quo or thrives in this disruptive age.

When teaching is viewed as an occupation, superficial pedagogical expertise is often seen as sufficient. However, this lack of pedagogical expertise brings with it a lack of knowledge, wisdom and self-confidence to make judgment-based decisions. In an occupation-based education system, teachers do not have the authority or autonomy to make important decisions; the role of teachers is to learn and deliver content at a standardized level, pace, practice and style. The lack of empowerment or ability may lead to a sense of helplessness and encourage teachers to 'pass the buck' to the next teacher or next decision maker without anybody feeling the urgency or responsibility to make the difference when our students face challenges or begin to fail.

In contrast, teachers who view themselves and are viewed by others as professionals have in-depth expertise in the content areas, cognitive development, learning psychology and pedagogical practice to help students learn. This expertise allows professional educators to assess the situation and make decisions to solve the problems immediately in front of them. Professional recognition brings with it the responsibility to make autonomous decisions to further each child's individual learning trajectory.

David Edwards, with a PhD in educational policy and leadership, is the general secretary of Education International, the federation of 32 million teachers and other educators in 173 countries. He described professional teachers as "illuminators of knowledge that have brought down fear and ignorance that has eroded democracy."[3] I see this through the work of my colleagues around the world and in my role as a high school history teacher. Throughout history the rise of authoritarianism always included the rounding up, public debasement and silencing of teachers as well as academics, journalists and artists—society's public educators. Why? Because teachers play an essential role in our communities as facilitators, civic leaders, moral guides, innovators, makers and advocates. Taken together, that is professional excellence in education.

To be successful at this momentous task we must, as I stated in Chapter 1, help every child fulfill their potential and flourish in life. That means teaching students in all their complexities and diversity to get them ready for the workforce, to be active members of society and to be self-actualized and healthy. At the heart of that statement shines through the definition of being a professional: trust, autonomy and ownership. A large part of being a professional teacher is the ability to build relationships to help everyone develop to their full potential. This means that your priority should be about getting to know your students and to understand how to make the learning relevant within their zone of proximal development. Building relationships is part of the profession but it is rarely, if ever, part of our formal education as teachers.

That requires a different type of teaching that provides teachers with more autonomy and with it, more responsibility for the success of their students. This is the difference between a profession and an occupation. It is important to remember the difference between the two is not a choice between bad and good. Rather it is the difference between good and great—and in our ever-changing world, that could make all the difference. Change leadership expert Jim Collins defined it in the following way:

> Good is the enemy of great. And that is one of the key reasons why we have so little that becomes great. We don't have great schools, principally because we have good schools. We don't have great government, principally because we have good government. Few people attain great lives, in large part because it is just so easy to settle for a good life.[4]

Finland and Singapore are both at the pinnacle of teaching being a profession. It wasn't always that way. In a 2017 peer-reviewed article, Linda Darling-Hammond describes how they transformed:

Teaching has become the most sought-after profession after medicine and many teachers pursue PhD's and then remain teaching. In a single generation, Finland leapt from a relatively poorly educated nation to a 21st century powerhouse with a current literacy rate of 96 per cent, high graduation and college going rates and top scores in all areas of the PISA . . . it is no coincidence that teachers are highly respected and supported. . . . Singapore has shifted from just getting teachers . . . to providing teachers of quality.[5]

During my time in both countries, I witnessed this professionalism firsthand. The structures, processes, collaboration and teacher leadership deserve this recognition. It is a bit of an oxymoron: It permeates throughout their societies in a humble way, yet you can feel the confidence in teachers to give youth a great foundation which is a source of pride.

Going from good to great requires no small degree of risk-taking. It will require all parties involved in creating a great school—teachers, administrators, parents, students and community partners—to learn to trust each other. To do that, we must confront those three underlying issues that hold us back: control, leadership and self-identity.

Control: The Central Tenet of the Occupation Model

As any teacher will tell you, just about everyone has an opinion about their local school system. It sometimes feels like everyone who has ever sat in a classroom is an expert on how to improve, fix or reimagine education for the 21st century. Teachers hear it all, at the grocery store, at family gatherings and from strangers making small talk with a casual 'what do you do?' Let me tell you: What we do is debated by politicians, critiqued by the EdTech sector and studied by researchers. So many players are all seeking the same thing: control of the classroom.

Parents seek control over their children's development. The EdTech sector seeks control for financial gain. The wider private sector seeks control to meet labor force demands. Administrators seek control to avoid criticism from political masters. And politicians seek control to curry favor with voters and demonstrate leadership. These combine to make the profession vulnerable to the fads of society, despite the expertise of teachers. While governments should articulate the purpose and vision for a society's education system, where things get murky is in who oversees the implementation. I say it should be teachers—the experts on classroom dynamics and student learning arcs. And in strong education systems, where teachers are treated as professionals, such as in Massachusetts, Canada and Finland, this tends to be the case. But there are troubling signs that teachers are losing ground to larger, outside forces that seek to reduce teaching to the sum of its parts in many other jurisdictions around the world.

There are too many hands in education without the expertise and reliable, ethical research from the classroom driving changes that are rooted in a belief that education is failing students. From my travels in jurisdictions around the world, these are almost always top-down systems where government doesn't invest equitably in education and the social support structures needed for education to flourish, where decision-making is driven by high-stakes standardized testing percentages and big data, and teachers' voices are ignored. When that happens, teachers don't take ownership of their work and approach it as merely an occupation. They shut down, worn down and jaded by a lack of control over their work and student outcomes. This can be caused by a number of factors including a lack of ongoing professional learning and one-off micro-management from school administration.

High-stakes standardized testing: Take for instance the debate over high-stakes standardized testing and the political fallout it produces. PISA and TIMSS (Trends in International Mathematics and Science Study) rankings, SAT and ACT scores for college admissions and other national and regional rankings are often used by politicians and educational bureaucrats to justify treating teaching as an occupation: A firm hand is needed to reshape the education system to get students ready for the knowledge economy. Countries and education jurisdictions can become preoccupied with high-stakes rankings as a means to draw a direct correlation between student performance and economic growth, specifically as it relates to the need for highly skilled workers. This often leads to a desire to control exactly when, what and how education is done. This way of thinking places the responsibility and blame of low assessment scores on schools and teachers without looking at the other social factors that influence the development of a child. This conformist approach suggests the only path to a good life is via the academic route. Basically, no other pathways matter, no diversity, no respect for all the other professions in life, as well as nothing on social-emotional competencies or civic engagement to flourish in life.

Teacher training: With the massive teacher shortage that will grow exponentially worldwide by 2030, what is the answer to this problem? For some jurisdictions, it is to make it easier to become a teacher by relaxing teacher qualifications. However, a system with less qualified teachers will revert to a more prescriptive, top-down education system, complete with regimented lesson plans delivered in the same way, at the same time, marked identically with a standard score sheet. Every child gets the same content and exercises, followed by a standardized test to insure compliance on behalf of the teacher and to rank the students.

Lower skill levels justify lowered wages too. Globally, some countries are veering toward teaching as an occupation with the permitting of for-profit companies to train 'teachers' in six weeks. I place the term 'teacher' in quotation marks because you simply cannot learn how to teach students well in a few weeks. Professional teachers, much like professional engineers, doctors and lawyers, require a combination of theoretical training, on-the-job learning and ongoing professional development in order to stay current with evolving pedagogical trends and societal needs.

Most disturbing to me regarding these quickie courses is that the trainees are often sent to teach in high-poverty neighborhoods or rural areas in countries around the world, home to the very students who need the specialized training a professional educator receives. Suggesting that a minimum of teacher education is required trivializes education by saying that as long as you have content expertise, you can teach. It's like saying that since I have read a handful of cookbooks and worked my way around my kitchen, clearly I am Anthony Bourdain's protégé. Motivating and understanding people are just some of the added requirements for coaching and teaching. These cannot be learned in a short, superficial treatment. This is the belief that education is an occupation. If this continues, it is a very dangerous road that can be automated and will ruin the foundation of any country within a single generation.

The big goal—our Mars shot—should be to have every teacher in the world trained and practicing as a professional with the rights and responsibilities associated with it. The reality is that in developing countries, many rural areas, inner city, refugee camps and many more exceptions we do have complexities at play that challenge the accessibility of having the full workforce being qualified teachers. This is a challenge that will take creative thinking, strong partnerships and steadfast vision. Being in this digital age, technology can provide some help in finding answers to these challenges while making sure that they are grounded on strong teacher professionalism. This could be in initial student content learning and foundational literacies to new ways of doing teacher education and professional development in rural or hard-to-reach areas. Do not confuse a first aid battlefield treatment with state-of-the-art emergency room medical care. Likewise, do not equate automated technology solutions with true teacher professionals educating students.

I can see why some politicians and sectors of society want to create this type of education system. It means one tenth of the budget, reduced education taxes and reduced wages and benefits, the latter of which is a prerequisite for attracting high performers to teaching. It takes money to get smaller classes and provide students and teachers with the proper support. An old proverb says, "a society grows great when old men plant trees whose shade they know they shall never sit in." This would mean vision in decision-making for our education systems. The opposite is a system built around control.

Consider, for example, if a parent came into the school to ask if their child was taught something that appeared in the SAT. The school administrator or district employee can turn around and say "yes, the teacher taught this on Tuesday at 9:45 a.m., as you can see from the records here on this checklist as well as this video." It's not about learning at all; it's about covering your ass. In high-stakes testing systems, no one wants to take ownership of actual learning because to measure that would reveal the superficiality of the system and its supposed checks and balances. By failing to develop teacher leadership, education systems can automate the delivery of content, assessments and marking. It is the old standardized system wrapped up in 21st-century technology.

It would be a bad day when schools use security guards to patrol 300 students in individual cubicles, each with their own computer, a standardized video lecture, and an end-of-day assessment. This would be advertised as innovative, personalized education because students have choice on what subject to study first and what pace to travel. However, the paths to each discipline are narrowly regimented, identical paths. My mind goes straight to *1984*, except that George Orwell's writing doesn't seem so far-fetched anymore. It invites a comment about the impact of technologies and their capacity to support dystopian societies through impoverished visions of 'education'—technological advance is inevitable but not necessarily benign. Teachers have to make sure that they are used for ethical innovations.

We are living in a time of paradoxes. The world's population is healthier and wealthier than ever in our history and yet we are confronted with incredible disparities. Communication technologies have made us into the most connected generation with the greatest access to information, and yet we have retreated into groupthink and the comfort of narrow perspectives and ideologies. We were promised optimism and are faced with anger. Technological innovations have ushered in massive waves of economic, social and political unrest, and the result is the rise of an angry populism that feeds on people's fears. However, I remain hopeful. Visiting teachers around the world has led me to believe we are on the brink of a counter-uprising of professional educators who are taking ownership of their fields and advocating for what is needed.

Leadership

Teachers play a large role and have an immense responsibility in taking ownership of the profession. Sometimes, even in education systems that do see teachers as professionals and build the system trusting teacher autonomy, creativity and expertise, teachers still struggle with understanding their positions as public figures in society.

But when we treat the education of a child as a series of check boxes, we diminish the impact we have on the student. It is no longer professional when the same lesson plan is delivered verbatim, every year, on the same day, regardless of the clientele in front of you. This was feasible when the only thing measured was content, but in today's society we are striving for much more.

Boston College researcher and *Journal of Educational Change* editor Dennis Shirley is a renowned renaissance scholar of educational change who has helped schools around the world improve teaching and learning. He defines teacher professionalism in his book, *The New Imperatives of Education Change: Achievement with Integrity*, as "being able to make judgements on what is best for our students."[6] This doesn't mean we disregard our curriculum or school administrators. It means we need to take what's coming from the top and analyze who is in front of us in our classroom to synthesize the right way forward.

Professor Yong Zhao is the executive director of the US-China Center for Research on Educational Excellence in addition to having many other positions and responsibilities. Considered one of the foremost scholars in Chinese and American education focusing on ethical assessment and technology, he says:

> in terms of systemic change, innovation cannot be implemented—it needs to grow organically. To harness innovation in development contexts, it is important to build platforms for sharing creativity, to maintain a flat infrastructure with many opportunities for collaboration and shared learning, rather than creating elaborate systems of accountability.[7]

He continues: "education researchers and experts should focus on inquiry and asking questions about the current situation rather just providing answers based on past experience." This type of innovation from the ground up can still be scaled by all within the system, but it should only impact our individual classrooms if we believe as teachers that it will benefit our students.

This is not an easy task, and it is a reason why educational leaders around the world are advocating for teacher professionalism. It's easy enough to duplicate and replicate best practice models for content transfer. We understand the "how" to transfer knowledge; the issue is the rest of the elements of a holistic approach to education, which has many elements of what I call the art of the teaching profession: all the intangibles and humanistic elements that we teach on competencies, social-emotional learning, skills that really rely on relationship building and reaching students at their zone of proximal development. Take Carla in the United States, who advocated for a student who was in distress over being evicted and came to her for guidance. After calming the student down, Carla found out that the student had an assessment deadline the next day. Having a strong relationship with the student, she made the judgment that any assessment at this time was not going to be representative of the student's abilities. Therefore, she advocated on the student's behalf to push the deadlines to another time. Her colleagues accepted her professional judgment and pushed back the evaluations.

Professionals constantly examine their practice and compare it to emerging research to help grow their teaching. In systems that help teachers flourish as professionals, time and resources are allotted to have them self-reflect, work in teams and experiment to try and reach every child. This constant learning is at the core of what 21st-century learning institutions must be. Teachers are the ones coming up with research questions based on what is happening in their classrooms. They are listened to and supported in the inquiry of how to better their practice and classes. Teachers lead within and beyond the classroom. Dr. Alma Harris, a well-respected education leadership and policy professor who has worked extensively on school improvement, particularly in challenging circumstances around the world, has said that "the formal leaders provide the opportunity for the informal leaders to come forward."[8]

The truth is that in many systems, we know how to move forward based on very good research, but we are not making room for teachers at the decision-making table. This creates apathy, anger and resentment among teachers, who disengage and run from offers of autonomy because they do not trust those making the offer. Strong, empathetic school leadership is required to pivot this workforce. Consider this example: The leadership of a school might decide that all teachers should examine their classes every so often and determine who is at risk, and if so, what combination of ability, attitude or circumstance is responsible. Having a deadline is important to make sure that this important task does not get lost in the chaos. A teacher who views teaching as an occupation will submit their list on time and wait for action to be taken. However, a professional teacher may notice that a handful of students are struggling. They won't wait for the deadline to submit their paperwork; they'll take appropriate action long before the report is due. A leader will know that their professional teacher has acted and has it under control and will just check in at the appropriate time. A manager will harass the teacher at inconvenient times for their report without knowing that the actions are already in motion.

Relationship with parents: Teachers need to collaborate at a higher level to be true professionals. We need to embrace the input of parents when they speak about their children. We certainly all know parents who hover over their children, clearing all obstacles in their path and protecting them from every bump and bruise along the way. They can be aggressive, vocal and time-consuming to teachers. I understand that helicopter parents can make it difficult, yet they do play an important part in the child's learning community. In a situation with a helicopter parent, teachers must make sure to have guidelines for proper channels of communication in order to include them in the learning process. Really, if you think about it, these parents are big allies because they love their kids and are trying to help. What is more worrisome is when you get silence from the home front. The more teachers embrace parents, outside expertise and help from an extended support network, the more it showcases our professionalism.

By being defensive and not developing this type of collaboration, the perception is that we have something to hide. Dismissing anybody's perspectives or sources makes us look less than professional. As professionals, our job is to take input from all perspective and sources to map the best way forward for each child based on our expertise without being bullied into a particular course of action. It is the equivalent of me dictating to a doctor the required medicine for my child's sickness versus him asking for my child's symptoms and prescribing the right medication based on our shared understanding of the whole child.

Brian McDaniel, a music teacher in Desert Hot Springs, California, understood the importance of collaborating with parents to develop their child. Liz (not her real name) was labeled as a troublemaker in the seventh grade. Because of her profanity-laden defiance, she was removed from every class except music. Brian saw a different Liz in his class. He championed what he believed was her strengths and sought out her parents to discuss with them how to continue growing her abilities. Having this meeting was transformative for Liz, as she heard Brian praise her talent as a natural peer leader with exceptional critical thinking and verbal communication skills. Developing a strategic partnership with her parents helped turn Liz around. She stayed out of trouble, was a member of the national choir and attained the principal's honor roll. Liz's journey could have ended much differently if

Brian hadn't made it a priority to get to know her as a unique individual with the help of her parents.

Self-Identity

We all know the stereotype of the bad teacher: a discouraged, apathetic and jaded hack who hates their job and the kids in the class; think Cameron Diaz's character in *Bad Teacher*. We might have been taught by one, we might work with one or we might have heard about one through the teacher grapevine. But while we know they exist, we also know they are not representative of the majority of teachers. Ted Dintersmith, author of *What School Could Be*, discovered this during his 50-state journey, which began as a project to document what he believed was a floundering, incompetent and unprofessional teacher workforce but turned into something else: a celebration of teachers. "It's easy today to dwell on the negative, but I was blown away by the positive things going on in U.S. schools," he wrote. "I describe a wave of aspirational change taking place in schools all across our country. I hope these educators move you as much as they move me."[9]

From my experience, this quote is representative of the masses of teachers; however, a small minority can truly paint an unfair picture that teachers must fight every day. Whether we like it or not, teachers are public figures. And when one of us makes a mistake, all of us are painted with the same brush. The difference with other professions is that teaching is always in the public eye, either from the media, social media or the masses of students who go home and talk to parents, relatives and friends. We have a duty to ourselves and our peers to present ourselves always in a professional way as proof that we are worthy of the respect we ask for from our students and society at large.

This can be difficult in the face of increased accountability measures and standardization. Both can leave teachers demoralized because, as Professor Yong Zhao points out, this model

> is obsessed with what children do not know or are unable to do. Worse, education today has developed various ways to speak about children's deficiency, publicly and loudly, in the forms of tracking, grade retention,

and sorting into different programs such as special education, summer remediation, and extra tutoring.[10]

Rarely are teacher accomplishments celebrated; instead accountability requires an ongoing search for improvements, which translates to teachers as failures. Whether it is politicians, the news media or other community leaders, the emphasis is on critiques with little to no praise. This is no way to nurture leadership or self-worth in a group of professionals, regardless of the field. This pathway has demoralized many in the profession and stripped teachers of their status, value and voice.

But if we are honest, teachers are not completely blameless in the current perception of our profession. For instance, social media has given us a platform and we aren't always using it to our best advantage. Often, seemingly innocuous, flippant remarks can negatively impact people's perceptions of the value of education and the job that professional teachers do. Teachers lose credibility as professionals when the perception is that we don't like our job. Social media is a two-way communication platform. It is not a private staff room. When you post a meme that says "Halloween is my favorite celebration said no teacher ever" with a picture of a child going bonkers, you're telling the world you're a glorified babysitter. Bragging about a snow day or publicly counting down the days to summer diminishes the importance and urgency of education—and your role within it. It doesn't matter if you are at home marking or planning; the parents' perception is that you have a day off and they are stuck trying to find a babysitter while making it to their job in a snowstorm. There is a real need for transparency and showcasing what happens in our classrooms to build trust between all stakeholders.

A Professional Life for Me

The education renovation that most systems need will take time to implement properly. No more Band-Aid solutions; let's develop a long-lasting prescription for a 21st-century education system. With changes in government comes changes in policy in education, but stability is what is truly needed for education to thrive in this knowledge age. It's going to take inspired visionary leadership across many sectors to make this happen. This must be done hand in hand with teachers as well as parents, students and private, public and nonprofit leaders to develop prosperous communities in all sectors. This will take leadership from all fronts to promote and uphold teaching standards while continuing to pursue the changes needed through research, development and innovation to bring our profession up to speed in this knowledge age. Trust is the key, as is flexibility, understanding and openness. Ownership of education with the ability to see and implement best practices must be our number one priority.

Trust teachers to do what they do best: teach. A common problem in all education systems is the way we nurture teachers' specific talents. Traditionally, great teachers get promoted . . . right out of the classroom. They become administrators or subject matter experts in department offices. And why not? If you're eager and determined, you've never been shown a path that allows you to realize your professional ambitions while staying in the classroom throughout your career. That has always been the bottom rung on the education latter. If we are to build a 21st-century school system, it starts with changing our perspective on teacher development.

Different teachers have different strengths, and we need systems that nurture those talents to enhance the whole system. Those with a gift for instruction need to see a path that allows them to flourish and succeed in the classroom. Those who gravitate to strategic planning should be supported in becoming policymakers; those with leadership qualities should be given the opportunity to lead schools; and those who are learners at heart must be encouraged to pursue on-the-job research and analysis to help others improve their practice. Similar to sports, the best players don't make the best coaches and the best coaches don't have to be the best players. You do not have to be a great pedagogue to be a great leader. Likewise, just because you might be a great leader does not mean you are automatically a great pedagogue. Let great pedagogues teach, let managers manage what needs to be managed and let leaders lead.

An education system is always fluctuating, always evolving, and yet never arriving because it needs to be a lifelong learning institution for all people associated with it. When leadership aligns the mission, vision, management, structures and systems with the professionalism of teachers, we will have great classrooms. It's a constant balancing act at all levels, especially when trying to deliver a holistic education (see Chapter 5) that pivots to developing all students.

Treating teachers as an occupation or profession is one of the factors that will decide if we have a society that flourishes around the world in this digital age. It sounds dramatic, yet I really do believe this to be true. However, I fear it is out of the control of teachers, apart from showcasing our professionalism, mandating that teacher standards stay high and advocating for students.

In systems where teachers are managed like an occupation, you will never have high-performing education systems; it is impossible. I would rather we engage and empower teachers, trusting them to find the way to educate our children in this disruptive digital age. A traveling version of Anthony Bourdain for education should see this professionalism come out differently in rural, suburban and inner-city settings everywhere in the world, but in the end recognize the excellence in an education that could never be one size fits all for the world. What stays consistent is teachers being professionals, finding ways to reach kids to fulfill their potential with supportive leadership and systems.

We need system changes and alignment of mission and vision to reach our classroom to make this happen. Systems that are centralized should consider the "why" and the "what" that needs to be done in schools; decentralization places the "how" to do it in the hands of the professionals. At the same time, teachers also have a responsibility to act as professionals and to support each other as we progress our practice.

We need to plant and cultivate the many kinds of trees now, even if we will not sit in their shade.

Notes

1. Schwartz, Katrina (2016, August 15) "Sir Ken Robinson: How to Create a Culture for Valuable Learning." *KQED*. www.kqed.org/mindshift/46055/sir-ken-robinson-how-to-create-a-culture-for-valuable-learning
2. Zaru, Deena (2018, June 8) "Former President Barack Obama Mourns Anthony Bourdain in a Heartfelt Message." *ABC News*. https://abcnews.go.com/beta-story-container/politics/president-barack-obama-mourns-anthony-bourdain-heartfelt-message/story?id=55761606

3. Education International (2018, July 5) "'The World Is With You': EI General Secretary, David Edwards Addresses Delegates of the National Education Association." https://ei-ie.org/en/detail/15902/the-world-is-with-you-ei-general-secretary-david-edwards-addresses-delegates-of-the-national-education-association

4. Collins, James C. (2001) *Good to Great: Why Some Companies Make the Leap . . . and Others Don't.* New York: HarperCollins.

5. Darling-Hammond, Linda (2017) "Teachers Education around the World: What Can We Learn from International Practice." *European Journal of Teacher Education*, Vol. 40, No. 3, pp. 291–309.

6. Shirley, Dennis (2017) *The New Imperatives of Educational Change: Achievement with Integrity.* New York: Routledge.

7. University of Massachusetts, Amherst, Center for International Education (2017) "Rethinking Education: A Conversation with Dr. Yong Zhao." www.umass.edu/cie/news/rethinking-education-conversation-dr-yong-zhao

8. Harris, Alma (2014, November 2) "Distributed Leadership." *YouTube.* www.youtube.com/watch?v=Yu2WpW8dC4c

9. Dintersmith, Ted (2018) *What School Could Be: Insights and Inspirations from Teachers across America.* Princeton: Princeton University Press.

10. Zhao, Yong (2018, February 2) "Stop Looking at My Bad Leg: Introduction to My New Book: *Reach for Greatness.*" http://zhaolearning.com/2018/02/02/stop-looking-at-my-bad-leg-introduction-to-my-new-book-reach-for-greatness/

3

BECOMING A TEACHER

My education degree didn't prepare me for this. It's Wednesday night of my first week of teaching, and I'm flaked out on my couch staring at the wall. I am beat in all senses of the word. I am physically exhausted, but I am also beat down in both mind and spirit. I am failing at the one thing I wanted to—needed to—excel at. I am failing at being a teacher, and I am only two days in.

Why? I had an excellent, extremely detailed plan written by the fantastic, experienced teacher I was replacing for the second half of the year. I had a supportive principal and vice principal, and I had classrooms of average middle-class Canadian French immersion students. I was following somebody else's plan, but I wasn't connecting with the kids and I felt horrible. Why? Because I was doing what I was told, not what I knew. If I was going to succeed in that classroom, I had to make it mine. The next day, I went to see my principal and told her my problem—and my plan. I wanted to design lesson plans that suited my style and that played to my students' strengths. "Do what you need to do," she said. So, Thursday and Friday I spent each class getting to know my students. I wanted to understand my students' individual motivations, to uncover their personal passions and to listen carefully for signs of insecurities and self-doubt. Understanding that was key to figuring out how to guide their learning.

In Canada, middle school is grades 6, 7 and 8 (ages 11 to 14). Those are the puberty years, which means teaching at this level is all about teaching both school subjects and life skills. Hormones are raging and so are emotions. A middle school teacher needs to be able to delicately but firmly guide a student to learn how to manage their behavior in order to be successful academically, personally and as part of a community. Imagine talking about fractions one moment and then gently suggesting members of the class buy some deodorant. That's middle school.

That weekend I canceled all my plans and I got to work. How was I going to get the kids interested in learning? Who could I bring in to help me? What activities could I design? I started from the premise that as long as I didn't screw up with numeracy and literacy, both I and the students would be okay. This was key, because I was teaching eight different subjects from grades 6 to 8. A lot of the students had told me they were really into music and art—hardly surprising for that age group. When they returned on Monday, I announced that we were going to spend the next three months creating a production of Snow White. For the literacy component, I started by having my French classes rewrite the story for a contemporary audience. In social science, we considered the larger issues behind the themes of Snow White and how they connected to the curriculum outcomes. I didn't have a background in music, so I reached out to my wider group of friends for help. A local dance studio owner came in and taught the actors how to design and perform choreography. Math didn't naturally fit into our Snow White theme, so I gamified the math curriculum, which allowed those who could to sail ahead while I concentrated on the students who needed extra support. Since I was teaching science to all three grade levels, I got them to design websites that would tutor their peers including video, blogs, activities and formative self-assessment. During those three months my classroom earned a reputation as being THE noisiest in the school. My principal popped in a few times, but to her credit, when she saw the students were learning she just nodded and let me continue. As for Snow White, my students performed their French-language version of the play before an audience of 250 family members and friends.

My colleagues during my first teacher contract were absolutely phenomenal, from content curriculum expertise, knowing the kids, how to build relationships, helping out with report cards, routines and processes to giving me feedback and constructive criticism on my thoughts for learning experiences for my students. They supported me throughout that semester. The camaraderie, professionalism and willingness to go the extra mile was not lost on me. It was a lesson in how to conduct yourself as a teacher. Those lessons from my administration, colleagues and students have been the backbone of my practice. Even after I moved to high school, I continued to personalize my lesson plans to teach the curriculum through the lens of my students' personal passions and interest while trying to support my peers as my colleagues did for me.

I am one of the lucky ones. Most new teachers either don't dare try something so unconventional as I planned or if they do, they may receive pushback from administrators, colleagues or parents resistant to new teaching methods. Starting my career in a great school culture, with strong, innovative leadership as well as collaborating colleagues, was a blessing. I firmly believe that a key part of my early success was the combination of my earlier career path and having started my career in that environment.

I did not come to teaching straight out of university. I had worked in the private sector, which allowed me to develop an extensive network, to work in a culture that encouraged personal initiative and that provided ongoing mentorship and professional development. That is not the reality of most teachers. Is there any more professionally isolating workplace than a school? A teacher literally stands alone in their workplace. Each morning we walk into our classrooms and six hours later we emerge, having cycled through a succession of students with different aptitude levels, learning styles and social/emotional complexities. And we do this with little to no on-the-job coaching or support in those first critical years.

The False Promise of Initial Teacher Education

Teaching must be one of the few professions that assumes the newly educated arrive fully competent and prepared to perform. While there are a number of education systems around the world with mandatory induction periods that build on a threshold level of entrance and allocate mentors to new teachers, they are highly variable in demand and quality. The bottom line is that education systems are built on the premise that a new teacher can stand at the front of a classroom and teach on day one. No other profession operates this way. No one expects a just-graduated lawyer to sit first chair at a trial or a new engineer to be a project lead. You build up to that by learning as you work and by observing more experienced people in your workplace who in turn mentor your professional development. But that model doesn't work in the traditional classroom, which was designed for an earlier time when a single adult stood by themselves in front of students.

Initial teacher education (ITE) does none of us any favors by continuing to believe that their graduates are ready for the 21st-century classroom the minute they earn a degree. Now, it is true that systems vary, and that many ITE programs have recognized and would argue that they are just the start of a teacher's learning journey. Yet ITE is often not seen as the beginning of our professional learning journey, but the end.

Teachers in today's classroom need to be ever-evolving lifelong learners who constantly self-reflect on their practice, incorporating the right research and seeking out the right people so they can reach students who need individual development in content, literacies, competencies, social-emotional learning and character. Even though there is a clear and high standard for student teachers to have acquired at the end of their ITE in some jurisdictions, it still isn't enough, and professional development must be deliberately intertwined throughout one's career. Particularly, the onboarding of new graduate teachers must include a more rigorous on-the-job apprenticeship. Some governments are starting to introduce an early career framework, acknowledging that teachers are not fully prepared at the end of ITE, and are not meant to be, because teaching is too complex and must be learned over time, in situ. However, I would continue to argue that it is not enough.

The expectations society places upon a high-performance teacher are numerous and varied, each requiring learning and practice. John Furlong[1] wrote a report that describes how school systems need teachers who:

- Have set high professional expectations for themselves;
- Are committed to the achievement of all pupils;
- Take responsibility for innovation;
- Relish change and help to lead it;
- Are able to focus on the needs of individual learners;

- Accept and respond to demands for accountability;
- Take personal and collective responsibility for professional development;
- Are able to evaluate and use different sorts of evidence relevant to the improvement of practice;
- Are willing to work collaboratively with other teachers and other professionals, both day to day and in the development of their practice;
- Are willing and able to work in ways that draw on best practice from across the province and internationally.

To date, most teacher degrees have designed ITE programs based on the academic and pedagogical expertise of in-house faculty with time spent in the classroom concentrating on practice differing greatly depending on the jurisdiction. This is no longer sufficient. Practical, hands-on classroom experience needs to be imbedded in the design and delivery of ITE, which means working teachers need to be brought into the conversation to have truly successful mentors in the classrooms. Now, most degrees have practical experience; what is lacking is a truly trained, master teacher coach. Yes, teachers are the experts on the practical, day-to-day workings of a classroom, how professional judgment is applied, how to select the best pedagogical practice and how to build holistic learning and personalization into lesson plans. However, teachers in the classroom get minimal to no training (it varies depending on context) on how to mentor a developing student teacher. In New Zealand, mentors/coaches get training over two years to support new teacher induction. This country is at the forefront of supporting new teachers. In contrast, in many other countries there is much, much less offered, if anything. This is a vital piece of ITE and should not be an add-on. Engaging mentors, preparing them and recognizing that this is a special position within the education community is key.

New Teachers: You're In, Then You're Out

Figuring out how and why school systems have a difficult time retaining new teachers is a good place to start. According to the National Commission on Teaching and America's Future, "50 per cent of new teachers leave the profession by their fifth year,"[2] no doubt propelled by our erroneous perception that teachers are fully ready once they have qualified for the profession. A lack of funding for schools, proper staffing, fair wages and little investment in support services are some of the reasons that could be affecting teacher attraction and retention. I believe another reason is the disconnect between initial professional education of teachers and the true needs we are facing today. New technologies, a loosening of social ties into the wider community and limited professional support combine to place pressure on new teachers who are ill-equipped to handle it—and so they leave.

My initial teacher education had courses and discussions on educational theory, the history of education, cognitive science, pedagogy, formative and summative assessment, content, learning disabilities, literacies, multiple intelligences, universal design for learning and some technology integration specific to my area. In Canada, student teachers usually have two to five mentorship opportunities in schools and a four-month intensive internship, which includes evaluation by your host teacher and a university professor who assesses you as a pass or a fail. For most of us, it is the final cumulative assessment before earning our B.Ed. and moving on to apply for our teacher certification. There is a probationary period and then you receive full tenure after a few years and additional evaluations. I am fortunate to live and work in Canada, which has one of the best ITE formulations in the world—and still I struggled. Even the world's best systems can improve initial and ongoing learning as teachers.

Take for example a teacher friend of mine who speaks about how his university professor in technology integration approached his university class. Two weeks were spent on how to use a Smart Board to take class attendance—the technology was a decade old at the time. There were no lessons on how to integrate mobile technologies into the classroom. The technology integration that was discussed at his university had nothing to do with reforming pedagogical practice, self-reflecting on how to use the space with technology integration to bring out competencies, social-emotional learning or crowdsourcing information from students to create a discussion from that brainstorming. It had to do with a bureaucratic task at hand and to try to make it fun for students as they entered the classroom. Now, this is not the norm and it differs greatly from program to program, which in itself is a problem. High variability from one program to another creates inconsistencies in the ability of a teacher to navigate technology software and hardware in a particular school. Furthermore, once you get to your first placement as a teacher, you might find the school doesn't have any technology or uses another type of technology. We have some excellent model ITE programs that integrate technology to enhance the learning concentrating on pedagogical practice that are device-agnostic. These programs produce beginning teachers who are able to function regardless of a particular platform, software or hardware. They won't use technology unless it's the right thing to do.

Teaching is both art and science. ITE does a fine job of teaching the science of teaching—the pedagogical elements that have been developed and refined through decades of rigorous academic inquiry. What no one prepared me for were all the so-called soft skills I would need to utilize or the patience and flexibility required to juggle all the elements that make up a day in a contemporary 21st-century classroom. That's the art of teaching and on that, most teachers are self-taught. The irony is not lost on me. This is what was missing the most for me when I entered the profession. The art of teaching that I was missing includes topics such as conflict resolution; how to develop competencies such as collaboration, creativity, critical thinking and communications skills in yourself and your students; how to network with the community; how to get buy-in from parents and student accountability; how to speak with parents; how to be successful in the face of weak or damaging school leadership; and staff room power dynamics. All of these elements play a large role in making the onboarding of new teachers extremely complicated and should be done with more intent. My period of practice teaching in ITE did help to develop these in some ways, but mostly haphazardly without a strategic scaffolding plan from my ITE. It was a by-product of being lucky enough to get a great mentor teacher. It isn't done with intent. Add to that school culture, bureaucracy, course load, navigating of resources and learning the curriculum—the latter of which can often place you in scenarios where you might have to teach subject out of your area of expertise, specifically in middle school—and that's a steep learning curve for new teachers. No wonder they leave.

Take Michelle Cottrell-Williams, who teaches in a majority-minority situation at the high school level in Northern Virginia. Well over two-thirds of her students come from different racial, cultural, social classes and religious backgrounds than herself. She grew up unaware of her privilege and has spent much of her adult life unpacking her "whiteness" to explore how it impacts her teaching. How much time is spent in ITE doing that? What about doing this type of self-reflection during your practicum? What about how to learn more about these differences while you are teaching? What is the impact? It took Michelle many years before she realized that she was trying to force her diverse students to fit into her paradigm of what she thought success should look like. She now strives to be a culturally aware and responsive teacher who adjusts to meet each of her student's individual needs to connect instead of expecting them all to assimilate to the type of schooling that happened to work for her. This type of self-reflection, growth and application in practice is the art part of teaching.

Teacher as Coach

My background did give me a bit of a leg-up. Teaching is my third career. I've been a sports coach, both paid and as a volunteer, for over 25 years and I spent seven years in sales and marketing for a large multinational. I guess you could say I am drawn to competitive pressure situations, which on the surface you wouldn't think would have all that much to offer me when I stepped into a classroom. Pressure to perform? Check. High public expectations? Check. When I started coaching at the age of 14, I was drawn to emulate some of my coaching heroes: NFL legends Vince Lombardi, UK soccer legends Bill Shankly and Alex Ferguson, the NBA's Red Auerbach and Phil Jackson, and NHL icon Scotty Bowman. I read everything that I could find on tactics, psychology, sports nutrition, training and motivation. I read books, watched documentaries and attended any professional development I could find on coaching. From that I learned there was no magic recipe for making a great coach. The best coaches simply got to know their players and designed game plans that played to their individual and team strengths: What made them tick, what made them perform, what made them crumble, when to put into play different scenarios, when to hold back, when to push. This is what I call the "art" part of coaching. Coaches, much like teachers, use formative assessment methods to move the team forward while tending to the personal improvement for all players.

Michelle, showcased just above, now understands that getting to know her students is key to move her whole classroom forward. Changing her approach to become more culturally responsive has been the most effective strategy of her career.

> Many of my students come to me emotionally malnourished; by the time they reach high school, they have already spent years hearing from authority figures that they don't quite measure up, that their best efforts just aren't good enough. Even though most children start their school careers excited to learn, the cumulative effect of negative feedback builds up feelings of shame in these children. With a system in place that has worked so well to convince a child that they are a failure, it becomes essential to help that student learn that failure is human, but it does not define a person's worth.

Through pedagogical practices in her classroom, Michelle is able to successfully create a safe, empathetic space for her students to make mistakes, learn from each other's differences and courageously embrace their vulnerabilities in ways that make them more confident, mature and strong. She teaches them how to be responsible for their learning and gives them the confidence to strive to be better in all parts of their lives.

During the first few years of my coaching career, I struggled because I was so young and thought I needed to lead with my voice, authority and drills. However, as my first group of players grew older, I started realizing that they weren't reacting to adversity properly on the field. I had built human robots who could execute the technique properly in specific patterns of play, but when the opposition increased in skill and discipline, my players struggled to understand what was happening on the field. They needed creativity, communication, critical thinking and problem-solving to succeed on the field. Successful coaches know the best path to success is to empower players to be the best possible version of themselves by putting them in the best possible positions—in other words, assessing and teaching players in that combination of technical tactics that the teaching profession has labeled 'competencies.'

When we are at our best, teaching is very similar to coaching. The skills, intuition and empathy combined with the use of scientific data that great coaches bring to their teams are precisely what teachers need to refine in order to move from good to great. Like great coaches, great teachers build relationships to understand when to differentiate pedagogies, when to motivate, when to step aside, when to let students struggle and when to hold them by the hand.

A Vision for Lifelong Teacher Learning

What is needed for ITE and lifelong professional development for teachers to work? First, we know the best ITE is a foundation for an ever-evolving professional career that is flexible, active and forward-thinking, attracting the strongest possible candidates, supporting the teachers financially during their student teacher years, developing a strong link between theory, practice, research and policy and correlating strong ITE to ongoing professional development.

Second, policymakers, leadership and teacher learning institutions need to acknowledge that we have different strands of expertise that teachers need to develop in order to be high-performing professionals. This means we should have more than token career pathways apart from school administration, which is often called school leadership or policy work. The truth is we should have more natural career pathways for our master teacher. Specifically, we need to provide professional development that enhances the skills needed to be a high-performing teacher, such as the art part of teaching as well as subject expertise, pedagogical expertise, training in how to develop/nurture relationships with the age groups you teach, design thinking, educational theory and student assessment. All of these are complex, ever-changing and cannot be mastered in one-off siloed lecture or a one-day meeting blitz.

This type of learning for teachers doesn't get integrated into classroom practice. No time to self-reflect means no time to implement into existing plans. Right now, teachers don't always get what we need to improve our practice, which is frequent longitudinal strategic planning of our professional development personalized to each of our needs.

We will get time if we take a university sabbatical to do extra training, but this oftentimes is theoretical and not practice. Furthermore, when we do take sabbaticals it's usually for administration, resource or guidance, which is all about pulling teachers out of the classroom rather than making them better within it. So you go back to school or get professional development to leave the classroom, not to master practice within it.

As we move education forward, ITE, teacher apprenticeship, onboarding of new teachers (which could be anywhere from one to five years), re-education of the current workforce and professional development needs to be renovated to make sure our professional ideals can play a large role in our communities, nations and world.

The first part of this renovation is to develop a strategic leadership, vision and plan for professional development. We need to develop a culture of lifelong learning among ourselves, understanding that we never fully arrived as teachers; we are always evolving. As professionals, we need to lead through our actions and our words in imbedding this culture in our schools and in our larger education systems. The second part is that we need to move forward with a true professional development model for all career stages. We need to agree as a worldwide profession on clear and precise standards on what it takes to become a teacher.

Education researcher and director of the Melbourne Educational Research Institute at the University of Melbourne, John Hattie, author of *Visible Learning* and *Visible Learning for Teachers*, suggests we need to develop what he calls collective teacher advocacy to develop a pan-professional culture across our systems, schools and professional collaboration groups. The influence of the collective teacher advocacy should leak into the initial teacher education to help us understand our civic responsibility, leadership role in our societies and the ability to be key players in the innovation needed in all sectors of our communities, while being an important role model for our students. Teachers can and should be the collective conscience of our communities, living, demonstrating and teaching our communities' shared values and beliefs and with our fellow professionals around the world, seeking cross-cultural understanding. A pan-professional culture could also increase the mobility of teachers, which in addition to supporting cross-cultural learning offers a practical solution to help address the global teacher shortage by redistributing teachers to systems that are in dire need of professional educators. In this digital age, many university classes can be done via videoconferencing and through the cloud. What would be vastly missing is the art part of teaching for remote, rural or developing areas. By having a pan-professional culture, your master teacher mentors can then travel and help develop teachers in these high-need areas, understanding the cultural complexities and nuances that it will bring to pedagogical practice.

Series co-editor Pak Tee Ng has thought a lot about this and writes that "a key way to build professional loyalty and beliefs is through the development of shared symbols and ceremony."[3] For instance, since 1922 Canadian engineers have received an iron ring in a special ceremony when they earn their professional designation; it is a practice that was adopted by American engineers in the 1970s. The ring is a tangible symbol to emphasize the burden of responsibility that they are undertaking by joining the profession. Physicians have either white coat or stethoscope presentations, while registered nurses earn their 'RN' pin. For teachers, the best example is Singapore's Teachers Compass Ceremony, where pre-service teachers take the "Teacher's Pledge and receive a compass, which points to the true north, depicts the various facets of the Ethos of the Teaching Profession and symbolises the constancy of teachers' values."[4] This could be a great, unifying symbol for teachers around the world to embrace our collective teacher advocacy.

Andreas Schleicher, the OECD's Director for Education and Skills and coordinator for PISA, often says that the greatest investment any education system can do is raise the bar on the teaching profession. This can be done in multiple ways, such as attracting the best candidates into the profession and providing the best possible ITE and ongoing professional development throughout a teacher's career. Given that there will be an estimated global shortage of 69 million teachers by 2030 (UNESCO), policymakers and local school administrators are scrambling to come up with solutions to this massive problem. Unsurprisingly, there are a number of quick fixes popping up all over the world, but these are trying to treat the symptoms instead of looking at the complicated root causes. To do the latter will require focused and determined leadership. Furthermore, ongoing professional education throughout our careers is necessary as we wade deeper into the economic, technological and social uncertainty of the Fourth Industrial Revolution.

A New Model for ITE

Current training models are not designed for the rapidly changing system of the digital age. This is new territory for everyone. Student teachers draw on their memories of a school system that, when they re-enter it as a teacher, may be different. Faculties of education are designed for research, which means few if any faculty members are working teachers at the moment. Thus, they might be lacking a working knowledge as a practitioner of what it's like to teach in a Fourth Industrial Revolution classroom. Again, this varies greatly if you look specifically at ITE faculties: You will often find not researchers but staff recruited from schools with strong teaching backgrounds in order to become a tutor.

Furthermore, teaching in this age is also new for the mentor teacher who takes on a student intern. We don't have enough experience ourselves to adequately mentor a student teacher. This is the reality of learning and working in an age of uncertainty.

We can learn from places such as Singapore, Netherlands, Norway, Canada and Finland, where teachers are held in high regard. However, making the job respectable isn't enough: Jurisdictions must also set a rigorous and credible path to meet teacher standards and qualifications for their systems. For instance, from my understanding through discussions with colleagues in Wales, they are developing a system modeled after a hospital clinical education with a mentorship, while Finland and Canada use on-the-job training ranging from a semester to a year before trainees can qualify as classroom teachers. In the best performing systems, there is strong communication and collaboration between the mentor teacher and the university professor in charge of mentorships/internships.

From classrooms and meetings with teachers all over, I have the following three impressions. First, teachers love to teach. While there are some who are interested in pursuing management opportunities or diving into research, the majority simply want to get better at teaching. Second, the disconnect between teacher education and working classrooms has been brewing for a number of years, and it is about to bubble over. We must move quickly to reset ITE so graduates are better prepared and supported for the academic, social, technological and political dynamics of a 21st-century classroom. Third, teachers want to help. I spoke with many teachers from India to Finland and everywhere in between who have great ideas for how to train teachers and support their transition into the classroom. Peer-to-peer learning sits at the heart of this evolution.

With all that in mind, allow me to humbly suggest the following model for ITE based on my experience as a new teacher and from the experiences and ideas of teachers I've met on my travels. It is a combined training program that includes an equal mix of theory, in-class practice and peer-to-peer mentoring that would conclude with a B.Ed., an enhanced professional practice designation and first steps into a master's degree of pedagogical practice, research, policy or administration. I would like to propose a model to start the discussion for improvement. Reminder that this is a suggested starting point. Readers should consider international differences, alternative pathways for people who already have a degree in a subject (particularly for older students within that subject), subject degree expectations, teaching in elementary school, and teaching high school students.

Years 1 and 2 would resemble a classic university program, with student teachers required to pick subject specializations. Here they would lay the groundwork for their practice through the study and research of pedagogies, theories and global issues in education. This is really subject content heavy.

Year 3 would introduce in-school learning. Student teachers would spend much of their time in a school being mentored by designated 'master teachers.' The student teachers would observe the master teacher's practice over the course of a school year, which would enable them to learn about the fluidity of classroom dynamics and how to integrate pedagogies into the real world of counseling, disciplining and inspiring students. This year would also feature cooperative opportunities outside of education for student teachers to learn more about the practical application of their subject expertise in the private, governmental and/or nonprofit sectors. This will serve two purposes. First, it will help student teachers begin to build multisectoral networks, which will help them in their practice. Second, it will enable them to understand how to prepare their students to be active citizens and to build successful careers being at the cutting edge of professions within their subjects.

Year 4 would bring student teachers into the classroom. Here, they would team-teach with a 'master teacher' and begin to design and implement lesson plans, counsel students and begin to implement their learnings. Master teachers would recommend specific courses to be taken back at university on areas of need for each student.

Year 5 would be for student teachers who want to pursue administrative and/or research in their professional practice. While continuing to team-teach and giving the opportunity to teach solo in blocks, student teachers in these streams would hone their research skills in the area of policy development.

Year 6 student teachers take the oath and become professional teachers after a one-year mentored teaching apprenticeship, having proven that they are fluent in all aspects of the teaching profession.

Partnerships between postsecondary institutions and K-12 schools sit at the heart of this model, which is a balance between theory and practice that would work intertwined in order to collaborate together. In this way, both education faculties and schools would have ownership of teacher training. Perhaps schools could be designated teacher training centers, similar to teaching hospitals in the medical field. Teachers within these teacher training centers would work with faculty members to design and implement a hybrid curriculum. With schools playing a lead role, this would provide a well-designed mentoring program for each level of a student teacher's practicum. It would give the student teacher the opportunity to develop practical school experience, be able to reflect on their practice and compare with other forms of professional knowledge. Bringing together all these important pillars of initial teacher education will enable students to reflect, analyze and challenge their practice while pushing them to try different things with the support and guidance of experienced teachers and faculty.

But it's not just the student teachers who need support and guidance; experienced teachers need training in how to be effective mentors and coaches. For instance, over the past two decades one of my friends has mentored eight student teachers and never once has anyone provided him with training or suggestions on how to assess student teachers, how to teach them how to conduct self-assessments, how to guide them in learning how to interact with students and parents, how to apply social/emotional learning to their practice or how to progress in their practice. How do you mentor others in how to develop professional judgment? How do you design holistic education opportunities for your students based on personalization? How do you self-reflect and improve on your practice? And how do you train principals to recognize who on their staff would be a good mentor for a student teacher? As I know from my years of sports coaching, the best performer isn't necessarily the best coach. The best coaches/mentors are good at understanding and analyzing communities, almost like anthropologists, in order to help new teachers grow and understand how to personalize learning for students. We need to be more deliberate in training.

Becoming Master Teachers: Ongoing Professional Development

Our schools and education systems are learning entities for everyone. This means that they are organic, living systems that are always evolving, which is why we need to continue our professional development throughout our careers. Like Singapore, Finland, Canada and many more, Wales has also been doing some very innovative work with professional development to make it relevant throughout a teacher's career. For instance, teachers are given opportunities to pursue research by collaborating with academics and outside experts within their classrooms.

Identifying and developing teachers' individual aptitudes, abilities and character would benefit both the teachers and the schools in which they operate. We need a more strategic, rigorous and thoughtful career development model that includes external partnerships and emphasizes self-guidance from teachers themselves. We must be the owners of our own career path. I believe if this happens, we will see a major change in how quickly systems are able to scale best practices and become more efficient in transitioning people into positions of

leadership. There is no one-size-fits-all model to professional development. Teachers are always looking for ways to better themselves and
engage in multiple opportunities for improvement.

Key to this is the recognition of teacher excellence through the recognition of something like a 'master teacher' designation. A teacher
interested in becoming a pedagogical expert for their school would
pursue a professional development path that would include original
research and applied pedagogy in service to earning the equivalent of a
master's degree. These 'master teachers' would then be in-school experts,
able to provide peer-to-peer mentoring and to be part of the formalized
training of new teachers. For instance, rather than the traditional professional development (PD) day model of training, teachers would have
the option to spend a few weeks, every two years or so, team-teaching
with a 'master teacher' in a specially designed learning environment
that allowed for ongoing feedback and self-reflection. 'Master teachers'
could also be contracted to produce videos and online training modules
for self-directed professional learning, which would allow teachers to
flexibility to improve their practice on their own schedule.

Again, I look to Singapore, which Pak Tee Ng describes as "one
of the countries in the world that really value and build the teaching
profession, in word and deed. It designs differentiated career tracks
for teachers and invests heavily in their professional development."[5]
Singapore's National Institute of Education (NIE) systematically
supports teachers. I am fascinated by the NIE's commitment to
emphasize career development pathways that are directly linked with
the classroom and therefore the practitioners. The institute embraces
a model of professional development that gives teachers the opportunity to have practice, research, theory, self-reflection, mentorship
and networks ready as they ascend to leadership positions. In addition, teachers in Singapore have access through their careers to these
resources, networks and expertise to nurture their development. Now,
crucially, there is only one source for ITE or PD: the NIE. It sets the
standard for all of Singapore, which could be challenging for countries
where education systems are controlled at the state, regional or pro-
vincial level, as they are in Canada and the United States.

For instance, in Canada most teachers' colleges are faculties within
larger universities, which means there are often multiple teachers'

colleges in a province, each with its own specializations and requirements. While faculty members work together on large research
projects and informally consult with each other, there is no formal
structure or process that links them. Unsurprisingly, there isn't much
pan-Canadian work being done in education apart from high-level
meetings, education conferences or national initiatives through large
nonprofits (NGOs). The regular classroom teacher does not regularly
interact with peers outside their province. However, you will still find
collaborative learning experiences within each province. Wider professional networks are developed for grade levels, such as elementary,
middle and high school teachers or subject matter or pedagogical
areas (assessment, innovation, practices, etc.) to get together and learn.

Formalized career pathways differ between Singapore and larger
systems, like the many in North America, because most teachers
don't have specified career development pathways from within their
school systems, which is troubling as we face down a complex array
of challenges brought about by the Fourth Industrial Revolution.
Having multiple players in ITE and PD in these larger systems has
allowed gaps to emerge because there is no national entity responsible for a national vision for education. It is still rooted in the old
industrial model of schools producing graduates for the local workforce. With so many avenues to explore in our professional practice,
it is important for teachers to have access to professional development opportunities in specific areas such as administration, school
leadership, classroom practice and policy work. We must become
more active in advocating for our own learning, such as pushing for
greater integration between teacher union PD opportunities and
those offered by the education department. When individual teachers are active professionals with major responsibilities for key aspects
of the design and implementation of their professional development,
we are going to see more teachers around the world take ownership
of the education systems.

The goal of professional development is to grow our practices and
make sure that schools run smoothly. So why don't we plan strategically
for this to happen for each individual as they enter school systems? By
creating true pathways that would be integrated with our professional
development model from ITE to end of career, we would have fewer

disruptions in policymaking, curriculum development and leadership across the spectrum, which would benefit our students.

Most of us simply don't get enough opportunities to work with peers in other professions to learn enough about social-emotional learning and character development or how to teach competencies within the confines of curriculum content outcomes. It will take a different approach to planning via design thinking to reach each of these pillars (see Chapter 5) while keeping each child's zone of proximal development in mind. This will require some serious professional development to help plan for all these elements in the classroom.

Teachers have been exploring how to do this for a few years on their own and have found some successful ways to do it based on their realities. These stories need to be heard; how they did it needs to be understood. Then teachers need to be unleashed to research, reflect, design, create, try and continue to implement the professional development required to realize this new vision of education.

Notes

1. Furlong, John (2015) Teaching Tomorrow's Teachers: Options for the Future of Initial Teacher Education in Wales. https://beta.gov.wales/sites/default/files/publications/2018-03/teaching-tomorrow's-teachers.pdf
2. National Education Association (n.d.) "Research Spotlight on Recruiting & Retaining Highly Qualified Teachers." www.nea.org/tools/17054.htm
3. Ng, Pak Tee (2017) *Learning from Singapore: The Power of Paradoxes*. New York: Routledge.
4. Ng, Pak Tee (2017) *Learning from Singapore: The Power of Paradoxes*. New York: Routledge.
5. Ng, Pak Tee (2017) *Learning from Singapore: The Power of Paradoxes*. New York: Routledge.

PART II
OUR CHOICES
AND OUR
CHALLENGES

4

DESIGN THINKING TO DRIVE CLASSROOM CHANGE

I have found many kindred spirits in classrooms around the world who are all honorary graduates of the 'MacGyver School of Teaching.' *MacGyver* was a TV show in my youth in which the star would always find himself caught in a death-defying situation with no possible way out, yet he would always find a way to save himself with a paper clip or something similar. It was brilliant. With limited resources, most of which was either donated, purchased through grants or 'reclaimed,' these teachers use their creativity, intuition and professional expertise combined with the science and art part of teaching to develop unique classrooms to answer today's problems. They are presented with curriculum outcomes and high-stakes standardized tests, but they still find a way with their entrepreneurial spirit to address the needs of students today. Every year, every semester plan, every unit plan, every day and every lesson plan is customized for the students facing them: From building for Habitat for Humanity to solving hunger issues in their community with hydroponics to designing drones to remove landmines, teachers are finding a way to create a holistic education in this digital age through design thinking.

Now, some of these colleagues, particularly in some US states and England, experience top-down, mandated classroom directives to make sure that high-stakes testing is the focus. Changes in education are usually preceded by either a change in government or a change in management, whether at the district or school level. It goes something like this: A new person comes in with the best intentions to solve education's problems. They are passionate and convinced that everyone will benefit from a new way of thinking. They are eager to see change, but they aren't always around to see their changes through. Maybe they got promoted or transferred, or in the case of politicians, maybe they were defeated in an election. It doesn't matter why they're gone; all that matters is they are gone, leaving behind teachers fumbling through the implementation of the newest strategy. Over time these situations add up, leading to innovation fatigue.

It took about ten years for the province of Ontario to transform itself into one of the best education systems in the world. How did it happen? By developing and then adhering to a long-term vision with proper checkpoints along the way that gave teachers the power to reform their classrooms to reach the outcomes. Ontario realized the power of a sustained vision from the top, removing barriers to free the teachers to design for their students. Doing this meant having stability in the classroom while still changing what needed to change.

True change occurs organically; this I have seen around the world. However, in the course of a busy school year, teachers can fall back on established behavior. It is natural to resort to the well-trodden habits and comfortable strategies of our past to deliver curriculum outcomes rather than the innovation that is needed for the students in front of us to develop in a holistic manner, including outcomes, competencies, skills, character and social-emotional learning (see Chapter 5).

So how does sustainable change happen in each of our classrooms? What characteristics of education are we holding on to that were valuable in the past but are no longer necessary? What characteristics of education are absolutely foundational and are absolutely necessary for the rest to flourish? I believe the classroom is the best place to create and test educational change. Small local collaborative teams can then evaluate which solutions provide the desired result and which should be discontinued. We need to allow teachers to be ruthless, within the curriculum guidelines, in discarding activities, assessments or processes that are impediments to moving forward. Developing the ability to judge what is valuable, what should go and what just needs time to evolve needs to be part of professional development for teachers. The critical thinking skills we are teaching to our students are skills we also need to determine how to lead effectively within our changing classrooms. We must choose to lead change with deliberate, creative, organic and custom-tailored solutions.

Why Change Is Necessary

Over the past two decades, educational change has been a top-down activity. A new policy, program or agenda is announced and teachers are expected to integrate it into their classrooms. That worked fine when teaching itself was a one-way street—the old 'sage on the stage,' teacher-centered model, with students sitting quietly in rows. But as we know, that's not the ideal model for a 21st-century classroom. Instead teachers must use a variety of pedagogical practices to guide their students' learning, which means they need to be able to adapt the day's lessons to suit both the students and the content. The teacher is and must be seen as the professional in the room with the content knowledge, the vision and the responsibility to ensure that each student progresses in an appropriate direction and at an appropriate pace. It's an amalgam of the old 'sage on the stage' and the newer 'guide on the side.' That nuanced balancing act is very important. Why?

In this knowledge-saturated age, our students need much more than content. Teachers need to think about how to design a learning environment that will allow students to progress through the content, skills, competencies and social-emotional learning in their classrooms. While students' needs have changed rapidly, for the most part educational change is just now in a similar direction but not at the same pace. Teacher education and professional development have only superficially touched on these momentous changes with ad hoc, one-size-fits-all "super pedagogies," such as project-base-only classrooms or STEM-only schools, and have offered no clear direction as to where we need to go in a clear, nuanced manner. As a system and as individual teachers, we are scattered and wandering, trying to keep up with the important and all-consuming work of teaching.

Here's a bit of the problem. Policymakers rely on measurable and quantifiable data to drive policy development, which means assessments and tests. In the past, these scores would be compared within your own systems. Now, policymakers compare within their own systems, but they put a lot more weight on how they compare to other education systems around the world which may or may not be similar in many ways.

As teachers will tell you, those results only give you a snapshot in time of a system that is constantly moving. One school year passes into the next and students move from grade to grade. Meanwhile classroom teachers rely on quantitative data but also qualitative data, such as the information they pick up by observing and talking with their students: an interaction in the hallway, a short conversation with a student in the bus loading zone, watching a collaboration, watching classroom activities unfold, debates, their body language as they come into class, the conversation you had at lunch and so forth. Individual teachers use these qualitative insights combined with quantitative data to make decisions every day for students. Yet, do all education systems value qualitative data like this? In my experience, it seems that quantitative data trump 'all in' global competitive systems, particularly when policymakers, politicians, parents and business speak about education.

Innovative Change Must Start in Classrooms

In this time of uncertainty, there is a need to test variations so creative solutions can emerge. When the system uses a top-down method to deliver a new learning strategy, there is a higher risk of affecting a whole cohort of students if it fails. This understandably makes practitioners nervous, and the end result is educational change stagnates. Teachers understand how to innovate in their individual classrooms. But what the education system fails to recognize is that what works in one classroom doesn't necessarily work in another. To be successful, we the teachers will need to take ownership of these experiments by applying design thinking concepts in our classrooms to make decisions on its validity based on our students.

How do we maximize the number of variations in strategies so that we can be ruthless in selecting only the best ones without simultaneously damaging whole generations of students? What if there was a culture and incentive from the top down that encourages classroom teachers to experiment and explore? The sheer numbers will yield some creative solutions, but the individual risk will be limited to small groups of students, which means it can be quickly adjusted if it is not producing results in real time. It is easier to turn a small boat than a massive ship.

Make Every Lesson Count

If power is to be given to teachers to design our learning environments and teaching sequences, there needs to be some guidelines to balance freedom with consistency of vision. Of course, in an ideal world there would be enough time to do everything. However, in a world where there is a very limited amount of time and energy and a whole host of objectives to complete, it is imperative to be strategic in how we use the precious time that students have available. Can we teach this content in a way that also develops a competency and practices social-emotional learning? In my practice, I carefully consider the importance of teaching something only if it touches on multiple pillars, or I will dump it. If I am addressing three of the pillars in my design, I will be able to develop my students more efficiently. It's important to make space in my practice to ideate, prototype, test and self-reflect.

Certainly, there are some pieces that are so critical that they have value in and of themselves, but this designation is only given after careful thought and not out of comfortable habit. There are some topics and lessons that I personally love and worked hard to perfect. They are some of my "darling" lessons. As my writer friend says, "you have to be willing to kill your darlings." After having carefully thought about how these lessons fit into the whole picture and how many of the win-win-wins they provide, some of my darlings have survived. Many have not.

It is easier to incorporate the competencies and social-emotional learning in elementary and middle school, where you tend to have the same teacher for multiple subjects. High schools traditionally struggle more with these ideas because of the content richness and expertise, the timetable and the silos in which teachers and students find themselves. But you do have teachers and systems leaders doing great things at the high school level by putting design thinking at the forefront of their approach to planning.

The design thinking process is one of many structures that teachers could use to design their classroom for innovation and lead change in their schools, taking care to keep the pieces that are critical and prune the little darlings.

Design Thinking in the Classroom

Utilizing this method to plan your year, semester, unit or lesson plan will give you the ability to think how to reach each child at their zone of proximal development for competencies, content, character and social-emotional learning while using the right pedagogy practice to personalize the learning experience. The teacher can choose when it's good for group work, solo study, teacher-centered learning or project-based learning based on the quantitative and qualitative data teachers collect through their practice. There are six interrelated elements to design thinking: empathize, define, ideate, prototype, test and adjust. It is all about constant testing, researching, producing and adjusting—with the student at the center. The design thinking process gives you the ability to plan and practice in a holistic way that benefits individual students, all your classes and your own professional development.

Design Element #1: Empathy

Apple's rise to become the number one company in the world was not because they were first, but because they were the best at homing in on the user experience. In other words, the designers were empathetic to what we needed. A deep understanding of users is critical in any user-centered design process, and education is no exception.

If teachers start our practice design from a place of empathy, we will be on the path to true personalization. This means putting ourselves in our students' shoes, getting to know them, understanding where they are coming from, understanding their strengths and weaknesses and understanding where their zone of proximal development is for competencies, social-emotional learning and content. Therefore, we need to approach the first few weeks of school as a time to build relationships and to create an environment for these elements to come out.

How many of us feel the pressure to teach a curriculum that is jam-packed? How many of us feel the pressure to teach to a test? This has been one of the key issues with policy from the top. It often backs teachers into a corner and makes us feel like we don't have the autonomy to make decisions based on what our data points and 'guts' are telling us.

As teachers, we need to be constantly balancing the answers we provide to students, parents and colleagues with our practice objectives for curricular outcomes, character development, competencies and social-emotional learning. How is my class for you, my student? How am I reaching you where you need to learn? Is there anything we haven't done that you think will help your growth? Each class has its own culture, with its strengths and weaknesses. We must understand our class and school culture from the students' perspectives because they are the learners of our designs. Creating the right culture is key.

The Teachers Guild is one of the leading trailblazers in design thinking in education. Co-founder Emma Scripps believes all teachers are innovators, civic leaders, advocates and makers. In Emma's HundrED.org keynote, she provides a great example of how designing with empathy comes from a social sciences teacher. This teacher realized after asking her classes some questions that the power privilege and race inequities were negatively felt by her Latino and African American students, who noted they received a disproportionate number of detentions and other disciplinary measures. It made the teacher ponder the power structure within her school, and she was able to convince her colleagues on staff that they needed to create a way to give these students a voice. After introducing designing thinking in their classroom content, teachers were able to create space for conversations about power and privilege. The result was that at the next student council election, the students elected a council with a majority of its members either Latino or African American—the first time in the school's history. This is a great example of design thinking at work in the classroom: to address a larger issue outside it that was affecting students' sense of self-worth and the overall school culture. It helped develop social-emotional learning, such as resiliency and self-regulation; competencies such as problem-solving, communication, creativity, critical thinking and global citizenship; and had components of the teacher's social studies class outcomes on governance. This was a win-win-win-win that all started with empathy. The age and capabilities of your students will determine your approach to designing the learning experience and lead to deliberate, nuanced pedagogies delivered in the right way, at the right time, for the right reasons.

Humility is the second part of designing with empathy. A teacher who is humble understands they do not know their new students. Even as a veteran teacher, I have to deliberately remind myself that for the students, they are studying this topic for the first time and they just might love it as much as I do or not. That is a humbling thought. For my students, I need to slow down, understand where the students are coming from, understand the goals of the students and ensure that they are ready for what I want to do. While I might know my classroom, I need to be humble and recognize that my students have backgrounds, demands, lives and aspirations of which I am unaware. It may seem like a distraction from what I am supposed to teach, but I need to find ways to get to know who my students are without invading their privacy. When I am humble and recognize that my class content is not the most important part of every student's life, I am able to set aside the busywork that can consume a whole day and concentrate on building relationships.

This makes it easier to empathize and then act in a personalized way. I can know which students I need to scold because they are five minutes late for class and which students to invite in when they show up partway through class. For whom do I enforce a deadline because they are lazy, and for whom do I need to negotiate because they are working a 40-hour week after school to put food on the table? Empathy for our students needs to be the foundation for all of the design that a teacher does.

Design Element #2: Define

Once you understand and empathize with your students, the next step is to determine what problem are you trying to solve. While there can be multiple problems to solve simultaneously, there needs to be a hierarchy. What is *the* most important problem to solve? When time gets tight, when you fast forward in time, what is *the* most important thing you are trying to solve? This will help you decide your plan of action.

We can use different teaching methods based on what we are trying to define. For instance, if a particular piece of content within a lesson is deemed the most important, you might give the students a short inquiry-based experience, lecture or assign a reading for detail and then evaluate their progress, all within a short period of time. However, if learning a particular process is the most important, you might behave differently, providing an example of the process and then allowing students to explore a similar process in a different situation. The evaluation may rely less on the quality of the final product and more on how they work through each step of the process.

Finally, if developing a particular competency, such as problem-solving, is the most important, rather than showing students how to do a math problem and letting them practice a whole worksheet, you could provide a unique situation that requires some thought first as a group and then a second problem as an individual, knowing that perhaps only a couple of questions in the content will be completed.

Realize where you think your students can progress within the pillars, and proceed to ideate the learning journey.

Design Element #3: Ideate

Ideating, which includes brainstorming, is usually the process which is most often poorly or too quickly done, but there is good news: Ideation can be scheduled and trained. During the brainstorming portion of ideation, it's all about quantity. We want to generate as many ideas as possible before pruning to the one we will use. At the outset, it is critical that the participants feel they are in a safe place to enable them to share without judgment—a critical learned skill for many of our students. There are multiple quick team-building exercises appropriate for adults and students of all ages to help develop this sense of safe community. For instance, borrowing a popular comedy improv technique that requires participants to says 'yes, and' rather than 'yeah, but' helps build common understanding. I sometimes have upbeat instrumental music playing, such as electric swing. It gets the heart rate going and encourages quick, popcorn-style bursts of energy and ideas. Other strategies provide quiet individual time followed by a group share process in an attempt to pull out individual ideas while respecting the collective wisdom of the group.

The best designed brainstorming processes have an initial onslaught of ideas followed by a break that ranges from a couple of days to a couple of weeks, so participants have a chance to let ideas percolate and conduct diffuse thinking. It is amazing how many great lightbulbs turn on in students' heads following a brainstorming session. Revisiting the brainstorming session at a later date is a valuable use of time to get creative ideas, particularly from more introverted participants.

The next step in the process is to eliminate. This is the time for judgment of the ideas. Take care to ensure that judging the idea does not lead to judgment of the person. Students and teachers alike are prone to attaching their sense of self-worth to a particular idea because they have invested time, energy and passion.

The urgency of solving problems often causes us to rush through the ideation process, in school and in life. Either the bureaucracy or our own extensive history with school often confines our ideas. Sometimes we are nervous about voicing a solution, or we do not gain the synergy of our peers because we are not willing to consume someone else's valuable time. It is the same with our students in the classroom. We need to create space for ideas to develop and to be presented.

Ideation comes with a lot of practice individually and as a group for students and teachers. When done properly, it can be used by teachers to engage and empower students to solve real-world problems with creative solutions while learning within their classrooms.

Design Element #4: Prototype

This is the details part of the design thinking process. Now is the time to break out markers, molding clay, calendars, spreadsheets, theses and PowerPoints. The amount of work to do in this phase can be paralyzing, particularly if you believe everything has to be perfect before it is implemented, resulting in anxiety and giving up. Engineers have a term for prototypes, the minimally viable product, or MVP for short. Built into the name are the requirements: What is the minimal amount that can be done to create a viable first solution? This helps to balance the need to implement something that is imperfect and incomplete, with being ill-prepared and unprofessional. The MVP should allow for flexibility, edits, modifications and further creativity on the fly as feedback is received.

How you define the problem will determine the range of pedagogies to use during the prototyping stage, and be assured: You will need to pivot to reach the learners where they are. The design of my high school modern history course is built with competencies and character development fully integrated with the delivery of curriculum standards (literacies) using a flexible structure. To accomplish this, I must be able to pivot quickly based on how students are moving through the content and skills, the state of their personal passion projects (the project-based learning at the heart of my lesson plans) and the emerging needs related to these projects as well curriculum outcome activities (papers, posters, 3D printing, video, PowerPoints, etc.). I am less involved in their projects once students embrace the problems and are comfortable self-reflecting and networking. The conversations become about 'how to' instead of 'what am I doing wrong?' This aspect of the class is often misunderstood and misinterpreted in non-education circles. This type of student-centered approach pushes the development of civic and global competencies.

Enabling students to reach different outcomes within the classroom together is calculated by the teacher cross-referencing all the pillars to see how to approach the development of each student at that point in time. One approach is to create a project where they have more autonomy, pace and choice intertwined with classroom activities that are student/teacher-centered. For elementary and possibly middle school students, the teacher would act as a project manager, ensuring each step of the process is being completed and offering assistance when needed. For high school students, the teacher acts more as an advisor, helping the student hone their self-directed learning abilities. To develop a true growth mindset, I'd recommend encouraging students to create three or four prototypes for a single project, adapting and refining them at each stage, before handing in the final result. This teaches students that all initial ideas can be improved and enhanced through careful consideration of feedback from colleagues, peers, teachers and experts and not to fear the testing and feedback stage. This is how we will create a culture of learning in our individual classrooms and across our systems.

Teachers can design to teach for the whole class or for individual students, personalizing their approach to each student. In order to avoid overwhelming students, it is helpful to work with your colleagues in the school to address student needs and avoid the risk of them burning out. So, when you design, you need to keep all of the pillars in mind, remembering that empathy stage and that students have lives inside and outside of your class. This means you are constantly prototyping and evolving as they develop.

Design Element #5: Feedback

Feedback is a critical last step in the cyclical process of design thinking. It informs whether the design is effective or not. After spending so much time designing, prototyping and implementing our beautiful creation, we are convinced that our effort has been rewarded and are tired from the hard work of the whole process. However, the more creative the design, the more outside of the box, the higher the risk of failure. Sometimes that failure means a small renovation and sometimes it means a full rethink. Either way, we are often so attached to our little darling that we are reluctant to seek out feedback for fear of what we may find. It is the quality of the feedback and the quality of the analysis of the feedback that will be used in deciding whether the design should survive and thus steer the direction of the evolution of your class.

Teachers need to be researchers who are constantly growing in their design journey. We need to be always thinking, how this is working? How are they progressing as a group? How are they progressing as individuals? Are they getting pushed to test their resiliency? Is this giving them the opportunity to showcase creativity? What communication style am I looking for here? What content are they getting? What content is foundational for their ability to cross ideas for their future? Are they learning what we had planned? How do we know? Have I used artifacts, conversations or observations to determine if they have learned what I expected? Was my plan to catch the people who did not learn effective? Was my plan effective for those students who have already learned it? The questions go on and on.

In the recent past, it would have been sufficient to use the results of a classroom test, an essay and a standardized test to inform how well the students have learned the content (check for understanding often); but now that we are considering that many students might know the content but struggle with traditional assessment tools, we need to also use conversations and observations in addition to different traditional assessment product. Again, this is more nuanced depending the context. Formative assessment and assessment of learning expert Dylan Wiliam says, "when teachers do formative assessment effectively, students learn at roughly double the rate than they do without it." He was a part of a huge movement that was very influential to push against that standardized testing which is now a major field of pedagogical development and research in the UK as well as many other countries. The problem has been embedding this movement with real understanding in the classroom, instead of using it to get results faster. As in most things related in education, the reality is complex, and a nuanced approach combining standardized testing, qualitative data, formative assessment, observation and conversation is needed.

Additionally, the other pillars that also include skills, competencies and social-emotional learning as major focus points further complicate the type of feedback that should inform the next iterative cycle of design thinking. As we progress on our journey as professionals through the competencies and social-emotional learning, expect to see more formal assessment tools to gather this kind of feedback. As with anything, balance your feedback. Just because something is formalized does not make it more valid. The opposite is also true: Just because it is formal does not mean that it is inauthentic. A balance is needed.

Determining what to do with the feedback is another careful balancing act. Not everyone will like the design, while others will love the design. As humans, it is natural to weigh the positive feedback more heavily because it confirms our opinions and validates our hard work. While the positive feedback is encouraging, it is usually not very instructive. Negative feedback can be more valuable because it is an opportunity to learn and challenges the next iteration to be better. We all have our 'darlings': the pedagogies, lesson plans and lectures that have worked well in the past and that we will use every year. Falling in love with your darlings is a recipe for disaster as a professional. Wisdom is required to know when to dismiss the negative feedback because it comes from a pessimistic person bent on tearing things down; when to heed negative feedback and adjust the next design; and when to kill your darling because of the negative feedback.

There will be a variety of levels of success as we use design thinking to develop effective classrooms. Learning along the way is inevitable, imperative and a major part of developing a user-centered classroom. While it is important to look at the feedback at the end of a design, it is also critical to use feedback in mid-stride. If teachers are learners as well, admitting flaws and failures to our plans will make the learning genuine for students. By doing so, we have served as role models for a growth mindset, knowing that what we produce is ever-evolving, that we are tired of our darlings and not afraid of letting go. Do not confuse things that you like or dislike with things that were good for you.

We as classroom professionals need to navigate through all this information from students. A teacher who never listens to their students will ultimately only get minimal growth and probably only for curriculum content. A teacher who always listens to their students will ultimately fail as well because they will get bogged down in trying to be everything for everybody, never getting the group moving in the right direction. It is a fine balancing act. Becoming professional means knowing when to listen and adapt, and when to say "I'm the teacher and I know where we are trying to go, so today we need to do this" in order for the students to develop.

Design Thinking Is an Iterative Process

Design thinking gives us the flexibility to pivot and adapt to the needs of our students and the curriculum. Take collaboration for example. You might have a great project based on students' feedback from their community. You have built a rubric together, but you realize on the first day of working in class that students have no clue how to brainstorm. The reason you know this is because within five minutes they are already on-task pursuing an idea. Now, if you are on a tight timeline and you have defined that the main goal is content-related, then perhaps it is time to be more prescriptive and skip the brainstorming to a more efficient way of delivering content. On the other hand, if the goal is related to problem-solving, critical thinking, communication or relationship building, then you might take a break, show them how to brainstorm on a smaller more trivial topic and return to the original task now that they are on the right track. Stopping the lesson, giving a mini-lecture and showing students how to brainstorm in this situation would be key for future success. Often times, the groups that struggle the most in my own classroom are the so-called high-achievers who have mastered how to be great students in our test-driven culture. They struggle with letting go, trusting the power of the group and so forth. These are all elements that cross my mind as I plan.

Mairi Cooper is an orchestra director and Advanced Placement music theory teacher from Pittsburgh, Pennsylvania, who used design thinking to help her students enhance their orchestral experience. After 15 years of teaching, she began to notice that while her students loved their day-to-day experiences in her orchestra class, they were not at all excited about performing. In the spring of 2017, a group of students decided to forgo the only full orchestra rehearsal before their spring concert. Her orchestra still performed the concert, but Ms. Cooper knew that she needed to completely rethink her approach to her program.

Two weeks after the concert, Ms. Cooper walked into the orchestra room with a shoebox of Post-It Notes, 30 Sharpie pens and one large question: "Why are you here?" At first, the students were taken aback. Was she angry about the rehearsal, even though the concert had been an enormous success? They soon learned that she seriously wanted to know why they were there; she did not want to keep the status quo with her teaching.

She instructed the students to answer the question on any color Post-It Note with any color of Sharpie pen and to post it on the wall. Then she went into her office that oversaw the classroom and sat so that they could complete the task in anonymity. This was repeated in all three of her orchestra sections until the wall was covered with responses. The notes were also left up on the wall so students could return and write more answers if they wanted. Then, as a group, they organized the notes into common themes. These themes (access, education, developing a wider audience and the sheer joy of playing) became the 'four pillars' of the orchestra's philosophy, the basis for its pop-up concerts and the purpose behind each rehearsal.

During the 2017–2018 school year, the Fox Chapel Area School Orchestra performed over a dozen pop-up concerts in addition to their its school concerts. From selecting repertoire to communicating with the venue and arranging equipment, each of these concerts was imagined, designed and run by a student. Ms. Cooper facilitated the students' efforts, but ultimately a student was responsible for each concert. Perhaps the most telling part of this experiment came in the spring of 2018, when the orchestra began its annual review of the pop-up concerts. The orchestra collectively requested and developed a mission statement, brainstormed more concerts and devised a plan for the following school year.

By December 2018, Fox Chapel Area Orchestra students embraced their mission to "foster artistry and co-operation within and beyond our community by sharing our passion through music" in over a dozen concerts at nursing homes and memory care facilities, children's hospitals and Veterans Affairs hospitals, libraries and the Phipps Conservatory. Through Ms. Cooper's use of the design process in the classroom, these students are learning creativity, collaboration and critical thinking while also taking ownership and feeling empowered to change people's lives along the way.

How many teachers have this type of training? How many professional development sessions have we been through that touch on single elements that are trying to be implemented or a particular pedagogy style without looking at when and why to use them? When our professional development is based on one item at a time, disconnected from the ecosystem, there is little consideration how it will impact all of the other pieces. I'm not sure that all university providers run ITE or professional development programs on this basis. Outside providers do—because they are linked to getting quick fixes. Teacher education in many countries from a university standpoint focuses on deep exploration of classrooms as complex social spaces in which contingency is vital as a teacher, but this flies in the face of government policy and simplified routes into teaching.

When you change one thing, it will impact all other things. It needs to be thoughtful so that when you make one change in a cog of the machine, the whole machine continues to work more effectively. Design thinking techniques address this problem, which is why I use it in my classroom.

Teaching Design Thinking to Students

Our goal as educators in the Fourth Industrial Revolution should be to develop students into becoming adults who understand how to pursue ideas, brainstorm with empathy, scale great ideas, chase the possibilities while not becoming a slave to their own darlings, and be prepared to pivot when required. These are the skills required for sustainable, honest, transparent leadership in our new, knowledge-driven society. Part of being an innovator is building on others' ideas, which is why it is increasingly critical that students become experts in design thinking.

Paulo Freire, one of the great education minds of the last century, wrote "the insistence that the oppressed engage in reflection on their concrete situation is not a call to armchair revolution. On the contrary, reflection—true reflection—leads to action."[1]

When teachers model a failure leads to success approach by showcasing their self-reflecting, it creates a learning culture and gives students permission to also take chances, to fail often and, more importantly, to self-reflect in order to succeed sooner. That's design thinking. This lesson is necessary in a world where kids feel the need to be perfectionists because of the influx of idealistic lives portrayed on their social media feeds. Not only that, education systems expect them to reach optimum scores, giving them the feeling that they are never good enough. This leaves them with many ways of feeling they are not good enough; they are measured from the minute they arrive in school. The idea that we don't know everything, that everything will not be perfect and that asking for help is a good strategy will assist in developing not only the growth mindset but also the skills to develop communication, collaboration and creative competencies.

Design thinking techniques are not a free-for-all. A strategic planning process is happening. Our quest is to co-create with peers and students and get as much feedback as we can, decide how we will improve on it, and finally share it.

Teachers Lead Through Design

Designing learning environments for students must live at the intersection of desirability, feasibility and viability, and it must begin with empathy for the learner. Professional educators step up into leadership and accept the responsibility to design learning environments that maximize the development of the whole child across all the pillars.

Some jurisdictions make it very challenging for teachers to design learning experiences deep in empathy for students. In an attempt at thoroughness, detail and accountability, they have created prescriptive, day-by-day curriculum documents that are expected to be followed. They have created data collection systems full of check boxes, with test results as another layer of accountability. The teacher has limited freedom to design learning experiences. This type of education planning caters to a standardized high-stakes testing culture. This pressure to perform on tests is real and felt by teachers. The pressure is amplified when the results of a standardized test has a direct influence on their wages, course load and resources. This fear will stop teachers from doing the right thing and prevent pivoting toward a design thinking approach. Time and time again throughout my visits in classrooms around the world, this has come up. Even worse, it is often times the "elephant in the room" of any top-down professional development to superficially address social-emotional learning, competencies or skills, thus negating any real change.

I started my teaching career believing that I held the knowledge and needed to transfer that knowledge to the children. Since then, I pivoted to believing I was there to serve the best interest of the students. I am there to meet students where they are and help them develop. It is a position of servitude. As you move up the ladder from classroom to departments of education, every rung higher on the ladder is to serve the people below in service to making the learning possible for students. Students need to be at the center of the decisions affecting our classrooms. The teacher is there to serve the student with empathy. This will require a major shift in thinking for some schools, districts and department leaders around the world.

Education is the single most important social program for the long-term future success of any society. The evolution of our education system at this point in history requires an ongoing learning culture for teachers and for students that supports grassroots solutions that can iterate, adapt and pivot quickly to meet the needs of our time. If our society and our students are to flourish as a whole and as individuals in this time of great change, classroom teachers need to use the design thinking process to create innovative and effective learning environments.

Note

1. Freire, Paolo (2000) *Pedagogy of the Oppressed*. New York: Bloomsbury.

5

Building a Holistic
Learning Culture

It might have been the day I balanced atop the piano that did it. I was two years old and a climber. Show me a ledge or countertop and I'd be scrambling up it in no time. One day, after a particularly active adventure, my mom's friend sat her down for a chat. Mom was pregnant with my sister and in need of support. Her friend gave her three pieces of advice for raising a rambunctious toddler: "Give that boy some structure, ask others for help and sign him up for some organized activities to run off that energy of his." My grateful mother did all of that—and my journey into the world of holistic education began. Of course, Mom and her friends didn't call it that. But they understood exactly what a kid like me needed: a creative outlet and some structure to direct all that energy toward positive outcomes. Mom put the right structure and processes in place with clear expectations of the behaviors that would be tolerated.

It truly was a holistic approach to my learning, designed by my mom—and I flourished. I played soccer and basketball. My parents very purposefully introduced me to music. They followed the same strategy with my sisters and brother, finding activities that suited their temperaments and interests. And across all these activities, my parents taught my siblings and me our family's values: Be kind, be humble and strive for excellence. My parents taught us well, just like great parents everywhere.

Universal lessons taught across a variety of activities and situations: This is how humans learn best, and yet this isn't the way we are taught to teach in a classroom. In a traditional classroom, subjects are siloed.

There's no intermingling of math with history, physics with language arts, or physical education with social science; this is not what we find in today's classrooms or schools.

From my travels through various school systems and in talking with policymakers, politicians, community leaders, parents, teachers and students, there is a general agreement this needs to change to suit our changing times. Education needs to teach students how to be adaptable, to be innovative, to be receptive to change and to collaborate, all while exposing students to different life paths and supporting them in finding their passions. They are not all written that way, expressed that way or even communicated that way, but at the basis everybody tends to communicate that all learners should be able to learn how to learn, be proud of what they do in life, be happy with their life and be an active participant in their communities. Sounds just like my mom and her friends all those years ago.

Teaching to the Whole Child

Learning to learn is the foundational piece for designing and delivering a holistic education to students. This is more than simply the acquisition of certain skills, content or competencies. I can teach children how to construct arguments, think through and around a problem, memorize vast quantities of facts and pass exams without ever touching on their emotional response to these lessons. If that's all I do, then I have failed our 21st-century learners. When they are able to make an emotional connection to their learning, I see children make the leap toward a deeper, more permanent and more profound experience. When we teach to the whole child, we give them the skills and abilities they need to be learners for life.

There's a lively ongoing debate around board tables, cabinet tables, kitchen tables and staff room tables as to what this looks like and how to implement it. If we are trying to develop adaptable learners in this era of economic, social, environmental and technological transition, our educational systems will need to change whether we like it or not. The goals of teaching have always differed depending on the jurisdictions. What are we preparing students for? To be future citizens of our nation? To join or develop new and different professions that drive the economy? To develop personal responsibility and preparedness? To capitalize on student experiences to teach the importance of success and the importance of failure? To use school communities, large and small, to teach kindness and social skills? We need to teach students all these lessons, coupled with subject area content, to help students meet the challenges in the future.

To accomplish this, teachers must change how we teach and interact with students, shifting our traditional role as the knowledge keeper/transmitter and instead adopt the mantle of guide, chief designer, cultural developer and leader of a classroom with a nuanced pedagogical practice. And yes, there is still room in this model for the traditional lecturer role. The focus is to help students develop the ability to learn how to learn, to be advocates for their learning with a foundation of these three overall elements: literacies (skills incorporated in literacies), competencies, and character (social-emotional learning). Teachers, researchers and policy developers around the world recognize the need for this pivot, which has led to the development of multiple frameworks that use different language to describe similar concepts and themes that categorize the requirements of the 21st-century classroom. For instance, "skills" and "competencies" are sometimes used interchangeably and sometimes defined as two distinct terms. For the purposes of this chapter, we have embraced the latter—skills and competencies are distinct.

In 2015 the World Economic Forum's (WEF) *New Vision for Education*[1] defined a trio of foundational education pillars: literacies, competencies and character. Literacies, which are how students apply core skills and foundational knowledge to everyday tasks and include language literacy and numeracy, scientific literacy, information and communication technology (ICT) literacy, financial literacy, cultural literacy and civic literacy. Competencies are required to solve complex challenges and include problem-solving, critical thinking, communication, collaboration, creativity, computational thinking and global citizenship. Character is the traits required to thrive in a changing environment and includes resiliency and grit, adaptability, curiosity, initiative, social-emotional learning, leadership and social and cultural awareness. UNESCO developed these four pillars: learning to know, learning to do, learning to be and learning to live together. These two frameworks are complementary and work hand in hand.

Helping students make this transition will require teachers to consider highly personalized learning strategies that enable teachers to blend curriculum needs, social and cultural expectations and skill sets as they design for teaching and learning. As we set out to design our digital age classrooms, we need to be open to evolving our professional practice. By creating a better picture of each student, we are able to reach them faster. Knowing where a child is at the end of the school year in terms of competencies, social-emotional learning, skills and curriculum outcomes, and knowing that this can fluctuate depending on subjects, would be incredible information to start designing the new school year.

Educational psychologist Seymour Sarason[2] was an expert on organizational culture, which is why he always cautioned that educational reforms will always fail if those leading the change fail to engage the culture of the school. We need to get culture right. It's not just a slogan or a list of words. A great culture is when you have an overarching value system that guides recognized systems, decisions, practices and behaviors. It has well-established norms of day-to-day behaviors that are visible at all levels of an education system. Valuing the human resources, treating everybody with trust, instilling a sense of confidence and cohesion to solve any obstacle—wouldn't that be a great school culture? When the culture is right within an education system, a school or a classroom, it is a dynamic place where learning is at the center. You can see it and you can definitely feel it. But it's extremely complex and a balancing act of micro-decisions every day that will affect the overall culture. Everything is connected. In order to lead change, we need to lead with culture and continually manage the culture we want.

When culture starts to go sour, when the gaps start to appear, it can become toxic pretty quickly. It doesn't take much for things to go sideways: Just one of those elements not aligning and doubt will start to appear regarding the sincerity of the lofty slogan that your school has adopted as its culture. An example of a source of misalignment can come from good-hearted and well-intentioned misinterpretation of the latest educational philosophy, pedagogy or practice without a deep understanding of the pros and cons. This happens often throughout schools around the world. The implementation that was going to fix a problem ends up causing unintentional consequences.

Developing a Growth Mindset

It is critical to have a growth mindset as part of today's disruptive culture, particularly that policymakers, school leadership, teachers and students believe their talents can be developed through hard work, good strategies and critical feedback from others. When this happens, people within education feel empowered and committed, and then they receive far greater support from each other for collaboration and innovation. Emphasizing the processes that get you to that point in a culture is key, such as seeking help from others, trying new strategies and capitalizing on setbacks to move forward effectively. The system becomes a learning hub for all, not just the students. Schools are centers of learning for everyone: students and teachers, but also parents, policy developers and community partners. However, the truth is that the growth mindset brings with it ups and downs. Carol Dweck, who spent over 20 years researching and developing the ideas around the growth mindset, says that we all have a mix of fixed and growth mindsets that evolves with experience.[3] What does this mean for educational culture? Just working hard won't make the culture advance.

I have been on many sports teams, and while all were hardworking, some did not improve or progress. We were getting praised for effort alone. But that is useless if we are not performing properly and working together as a unit. In the end, some of those teams imploded because when confronted with obstacles, we weren't able to perform. My learning from that experience is this: Outcomes matter. Unproductive effort is never a good thing. It's critical to reward not just effort but also learning and progress. As Dweck writes in the *Harvard Business Review*, in "all of our research, the outcome—the bottom line—follows from deeply engaging in these processes."[4] Hollow praise does not help build the right culture or growth mindset. You must make the hard decision that sometimes might sting or be hard to hear, but in the long run it will help your students and/or colleagues reach their goal.

Building Culture in a Class, School or System

Culture is multilayered, and all of it impacts learning. There are three levels I want to address specifically—behavior, processes and practice—which have played an important role in my adoption of the growth mindset in my professional practice.

A positive workplace will have a higher degree of teacher engagement, and that will impact the response to initiatives coming from school leadership or systems leadership and have more innovation and solutions coming from the ground up on objectives or issues facing the system or school. When school culture shifts down, it is often reflected through teachers' lack of willingness to participate in any initiatives and lead to possibly detaching oneself from the work environment altogether.

Here are some questions to consider. Are your students looking forward to learning? Are they going to school? Does everyone in the school—students, teachers and administrators—feel an ownership for learning? Are they dedicated to it? What are they articulating? What would they say about the education culture? Are they speaking the school lingo? What would they say are areas of strengths and weaknesses? How would they assess the leadership in creating the culture? Do they agree with the mission?

Not everybody wants to ask those questions. Not everybody wants to face the realities. Culture is not easy to change. It is easier to ignore, to maintain the status quo. It is hard to constantly analyze, test, seek feedback and adjust. But if you don't ask, you will fail in implementing a growth mindset in your class or school, and that will negatively impact student learning.

Heidi Crumrine, an English teacher in Concord, New Hampshire, since 2004, recognizes the importance in building the right culture. She says that

> academics mean nothing without connections in the classroom. It takes work and it often means giving more than we receive as teachers. Sometimes the return on investment is slow, but it almost always happens, and it is always worth it.

One of Crumrine's favorite ways to connect with her students is by sending them notes of encouragement to their home addresses at some point in the year. She has a method. She keeps track of when and to whom she sends each note, trying to send them when students are either struggling with something or have just overcome some kind of challenge. At the beginning of the year she tries to target students for whom school does not come easily. She waits to send notes to the high-achieving students until later in the year when she knows they might be feeling overwhelmed and anxious with how hard school feels.

Crumrine explains:

> I always hand write; I am always positive. To my introverted students, I will say something like "I want you to know that even though you are quiet, I can see you following along and paying attention." To my reluctant learners, it will be something like "I know that coming to school is hard for you, but I am so glad to see you when you are here."

Simple words of encouragement have the potential to transform so much for a student when done at the right time for the right reasons. Crumrine adds:

> As our society becomes increasingly polarized through hate crimes, mass shootings, and overall division, it is increasingly important that as educators we step up to developing relationships with our students and engaging them in these small moments of humanity can make a big difference.

Nurturing the right culture is hard, it takes effort and time. Culture takes time to define. It takes work to execute. However, if your values and behaviors are clear and transparent, if you design and implement processes that reinforce the culture, and if you shape your professional practice to be collaborative and supportive, you will be able to build a great classroom and school culture.

Behavior

Everyone is a stakeholder in education. Creating the right culture means extending it beyond the four walls of a classroom or school and into the homes, businesses and volunteer organizations where our students live, work and play. One of the real tests of any value statement is how the leaders behave. People watch everything leaders do.

In my travels, I was fascinated by how Finns spoke about their education system. At the Helsinki Education Week and the HundrED Education Innovation Summit, I had the chance to hear the Minister of Education, the mayor of Helsinki, businesspeople, teachers, principals and students speak about their education system using similar language and passion. They recognized that each school's path would be unique to the needs of their local students, but they were all committed to making every school a great school. In Finland, everyone accepts their responsibility to make their local school great. That's shared behavior and it is powerful. Andreas Schleicher, as the Director for Education and Skills at the OECD, is one of the most recognized leaders in education. He writes in *World Class: How to Build a 21st-Century School System*:

> Finnish leaders empower their teachers by trusting them, and in doing so they create a virtuous circle of productivity and innovative learning environments. In turn, the high level of policy coherence, meaning that decisions will be followed through across electoral cycles and political administrations, leads to Finnish teachers' trust in their education leaders: they trust their leaders' integrity and count on their capacity to do what they say.[5]

Despite government changes, educators are trusted to do what is right, which makes education apolitical. How many systems have that type of cultural buy-in from the top down? Not too many, from what I have seen.

In too many jurisdictions, including many in North America, too many politicians use education as a pawn to garner votes, spinning statistics and data to fit their argument. These sensationalized stories play a major role in the culture of education that has taken root in our communities. It is assumed that all of the education systems are broken, and this belief is reflected in kitchen table conversations, rants and negative story lines that students and teachers hear—and bring with them to school. How does it feel to go to work in an institution that faces a constant barrage of criticism, where the practitioners are told repeatedly by political leaders, media commentators, parents and businesspeople that they aren't good enough, they can't learn and they don't know what they're doing? Ask a teacher and they'll tell you. We are playing a dangerous game with our children's future when we polarize education.

Furthermore, politicians and celebrities reinforce this culture of negativity through their behavior with each other. The anger, insults and bullying that have become commonplace in the public space sets a horrible example for our students. How public figures—be they politicians, sports stars or celebrities—behave, debate, collaborate and talk with each other has a major impact on our classrooms. Cumulatively, this public culture of outrage and bullying is not healthy or helpful in building strong, high-functioning and empathetic students—qualities that are required to be successful in the Fourth Industrial Revolution.

What are the expected behaviors we want from staff, teachers, parents and students? Have we clearly defined them? Do they reflect the shared culture of our community and our school? Accountability becomes easier and success becomes easier if you have clearly defined expectations of behavior. People want clarity, and in this age of change, it takes leaders who understand the group's vision, mission and work to uphold it with their words and actions. Remember, the leadership is there to serve teachers, who serve the students.

Negative energy zaps creativity, curiosity and empowerment in the classroom, making it difficult for students to embrace rather than fear failure. Good teaching comes with a sense of vitality, an energy, because positivity breeds success. Teachers need to see past momentary setbacks, analyze why they occurred and get students back on the path toward their goal. When students understand that your critical feedback is helping them improve and that your praise is used authentically, it solidifies a strong relationship between teacher and student based on trust. This type of behavior creates the right type of culture for risk-taking, so don't be afraid to show your own vulnerability, to laugh at yourself and admit when you've goofed, and then reset and keep going. Students need role models who are not afraid to showcase their vulnerabilities, because it is in understanding our weaknesses that we can develop our strengths.

Processes

To bring change to your classroom or school, the processes you use must align with your school community's values and behaviors. Those of you in some North American jurisdictions may look to Finland

and Singapore as models of education success, but if all we do is implement superficial solutions without making the necessary deeper changes to our education cultures, such as recognizing and rewarding teacher professionalism, our reforms will fall short. I believe there are five key process improvements required to create and maintain a culture of learning and growth in our schools.

Teacher training: We explored in Chapter 3 the onboarding process for new teachers and ongoing professional development, which must be revamped to create and nurture a lifelong culture of professional learning and excellence. Teachers need professional development opportunities that are tailored to teaching us how to teach to the whole child. I believe that teachers have always developed competencies and social-emotional learning in their students, but mostly haphazardly and not necessarily with intent. I know that I could use some help understanding how to better integrate social-emotional learning into my high school classroom.

I see the work that my preschool daughter does at day care within the early childhood education curriculum when it comes to social-emotional learning, and I wonder why we don't work with that type of intent in high school. While I was writing this book, she was learning about the different types of emotions, what she believes are the facial expressions that she conveys when experiencing those emotions, and how to voice how she feels. They even watched the Pixar film *Inside/ Out* and followed up with a class discussion. In day care. This is true social-emotional learning. I wondered, as I listened to her describe her day, how I could introduce similar teachings to my high school students, an age of high emotion and anxiety for most people. I have tried looking at self-reflection videos with specific questions to bring students to self-evaluate anxiety, resiliency and happiness through a semester-long project cycle. Trying to get them to understand when they can produce and be efficient, when they need to seek help, when to go out for a walk and so forth. Like most teachers, this wasn't part of my initial teacher education, and I seek the possibility of growth in my pedagogical practice to better design learning experiences to reach my students. Right now, I'm learning by trying—just like many of my peers. Imagine what we might accomplish if education systems set out with great purpose and urgency with the time necessary to train teachers in how to teach these 21st-century competencies and character traits.

One person who has inspired me to continue is Brice Hostutler, a director for the Pennsylvania Teachers Advisory Committee and a national board-certified teacher in Pittsburgh. As a therapeutic teacher, he serves students with both special education and mental health diagnoses. Many of his students also have a history of experiencing trauma such as violence, abuse and neglect. School is often the last thing on his students' minds, and yet they arrive every day. One of the reasons he believes his students have such good attendance is because the classroom is a safe space away from the realness of their lives. His classroom is a space where students can embrace the good in their lives without ignoring the dark places. It is also a place where every day is treated as a new day. Brice works hard to instill in his students that we all make mistakes, and that learning from those mistakes is always the best response. When working with students, especially those who have a history of not performing well in school, it is important to shift our mindsets as teachers from a strictly academic focus to one that really looks at the entire student, specifically the way that students view the educational process and the basis they bring into the classroom. These small observations are often the data points that make a huge difference in the lives of so many students but so often are overlooked or ignored in a world standardized test scores and predictive assessments.

Strategic planning: Oftentimes new processes land in teachers' inboxes unannounced and with little fanfare; other times they are telegraphed through political campaigns. It doesn't matter how they arrive; if teachers don't feel they were adequately consulted or engaged prior to a change, they are unlikely to embrace it. It will be one more process improvement that contributes to our innovation fatigue. To avoid that, teachers must be invited into the decision-making process through the implementation of ongoing, transparent strategic planning and goal-setting. Bring teachers into the conversation, particularly within each school, and we will accept ownership of the new goals and help implement adoption with our colleagues. The long-term vision of strategic planning needs to be designed from the leaders. What makes a great plan is listening to the people on the ground who will need to implement that vision. This type of strategic planning allows a degree of flexibility in how it will be implemented, based on individual school culture. Opening the lines of communication to make sure that the "how" is working, continuing to self-analyze and look to improve based on a clear concise effort will push the culture toward a positive growth mindset.

Assessment/auditing: A well-performing system or district could still have poor performing schools if the school leadership isn't able to clarify expectations or use feedback. If there is a lack clarity of the expected behaviors, it will create a culture of mistrust and fear. How many school systems are based in this manner today? How is feedback received from teachers, school leadership, department leadership? What do they do with the feedback? I visited a school in the United States that was using data from high-stakes standardized testing to give out the teacher timetable for the next year. The teachers who achieved the best results got the preferred placement and classes. That form of assessment created a toxic, competitive culture among the staff, with some cheating to get a better course load. School leadership created the wrong structures and processes that amplified this disgusting culture within a school. Rather than creating a growth mindset, it solidified a fixed mindset, as teachers stopped innovating for fear it would impact testing and, in turn, have a negative impact on their career.

Engagement: To drive a growth mindset, teachers need to believe the professional development and feedback they receive is relevant to their practice and professional development. When they do, it contributes to a positive classroom and school culture. But how many teachers believe that the professional development offered by their schools, districts and systems is irrelevant for what they need at that moment in their class? Developing the elements to a thriving culture means engaging directly with teachers to determine what supports they need to be successful.

Recognition: Set clear and transparent guidelines for recognition and professional rewards, and a positive culture will follow. Teachers are carefully watching and judging the actions of administrators and policymakers, which means every decision is scrutinized and has an impact on the culture. How are principals and vice principals chosen?

Do teachers perceive the promotion process to be fair and reflective of school culture? One school I visited had this problem. Teachers perceived that promotions into mentorship and coaching roles were given, not to the most qualified, but as a way to get worn-out teachers out of the classroom. It was creating a toxic environment. The solution is to create a system of rewards and recognition that is transparent and aligned with the culture of the school.

Practice

In *Teaching in the Fourth Industrial Revolution: Standing at the Precipice*, I introduced a process I developed for my classroom practice that I call Teach ME. As I wrote then, "no matter what happens on the outside of your class, a teacher can always create a positive culture for the growth mindset within their class." For me, this means a high degree of personalization, a term that in the last few years has developed two, somewhat contradictory definitions. Let's call it the human versus machine dichotomy.

One definition uses personalization to define the method of construction. It embraces the values of humanism by using a variety of pedagogies and teaching styles to develop a student's character, competencies, skills and core knowledge. Context is key, and it is the job of professional educators to determine how best to personalize their students' learning journey based on local culture, relationships and capacity. What works for me in my Canadian classroom might not work for a teacher in Seoul or rural Chile. Likewise, how I teach my high school students will vary greatly from how my friend teaches third grade.

The other definition uses personalization to define the method of instruction. It emphasizes the values of student self-directed learning using technologies, such as artificial intelligence and machine learning, to help guide students through a series of lessons at their own pace. The personalization comes into play because the student is able to self-select what course they want to learn and the speed at which they learn it. This is a glorified version of transfer of knowledge by a video lecture, pedagogical approach with standardized worksheet and assessment. It is disguised personalization. There is a place for this to help teachers, but it should not be the model for personalization.

It should come as little surprise that I hew closer to the first definition. While I am a big fan of integrating new technologies into my classroom practice, I believe strongly that teachers have a critical role to play in preparing our students for the world that awaits them. Critical thinking, collaboration, communications, creativity and other competencies are not abilities that can be learned from a machine. These are human traits and we learn how to use them best when we interact with others in a holistic manner. We are social creatures and we learn through modelling our behavior after others, self-reflection and group interaction.

I offer an in-depth exploration of the pros and cons of these two definitions of personalization in *Teaching in the Fourth Industrial Revolution: Standing at the Precipice* along with a detailed description of Teach ME, my guide to personalization in the classroom. The Teach ME model can help teachers prepare students for a world in which they will work and live among people of diverse cultural, religious and racial origins who may hold different worldviews. It provides teachers with a holistic approach to designing student development, learning and assessment. Through its various iterations, I have concluded that what works best is to engage students in competencies and character development via their interests and/or passions, linking it up to the curriculum. I get to know individual students on a deeper level, meet them in their zones of proximal development, and challenge students' existing paradigms to help guide their development. It is a work in progress, so please take it and make it your own, adapting it to your circumstances and cultures. The Teach ME development of culture model is presented here as a starting point.

Teach ME: My Three-Step Practical Guide to Culture Change in the Classroom

Action 1—Go Slow to Go Fast

This is a nod to my strong belief in putting the work in to develop relationships with my students first, and then diving into the curriculum. In practical terms, this means I go slow in the first three weeks of a new school year as I get to know my students, and together, we get to know their preferred learning strategies. Doing that means we can accelerate their learning through personalization that caters to their strengths while developing the whole class. It is quite the balancing act! Here's where my experience as a camp counselor and sports coach comes in handy, because I use a lot of the classic icebreaker games and challenges as ways to observe how my students process information, work with others and deal with challenges. I learn a lot from these games, just as I used to learn a lot from my players while observing them during practice and team-building exercises; it also helps build trust between me and my students. This allows me to understand where the zone of proximal development is for each of my students as it relates to competencies, skills and curriculum content outcomes, and social-emotional learning.

A teacher who I have profound respect for in how he does this with his kids is Sean Bellamy, a teacher at Sands School in England. He offers a great example of how to get to know your students and build relationships. Bellamy has strong foundational knowledge of pedagogical practice, social-emotional learning progressions and competencies development. With a lot of self-reflection, he came up with a model that centers learning around an emotional connection to the people and material via debate, a range of media and experiential learning outside the classroom. This includes helping to run the school, including determining school rules collectively.

"Adults are often afraid that if they allow children to choose between learning and leisure they will always choose leisure. And, that will happen, they will choose leisure for a while," he says, adding they need to come to learning on their own terms and to take responsibility for it.

> If this requires them to step away from class for a while to unlearn previous habits or to challenge their motivations, then we feel that the loss of a few weeks of education is more than compensated for by the sincerity of their engagement on their return.

Action 2—Challenge Paradigms

After the fun and challenge activities of those first few weeks, we are ready to dive into risk-taking and pushing learning boundaries. This period usually takes about four weeks, and I design it based on the observations and theories I developed about each student during the relationship-building exercises. I guide them through a series of lessons and activities based on curriculum outcomes for that subject, designed to challenged their assumptions and force them to consider multiple perspectives. Just as in the first action, I do not provide students with marks in this second action, just constructive criticism; this can add to student frustration, particularly among traditional high performers. This can be a difficult and troubling part of the learning curve for students who have been trained to 'write to the test' and view ignorance as a personal weakness and failure. To help them pass through this phase, I encourage my students to create video journals and written reflections of how they feel and what they think, which I review. This adds to my understanding of their learning trajectories and styles. If you've done the 'go slow to go fast' stage correctly, students will trust you enough to share their feelings of failure and inadequacies in their journals, allowing you to deepen your professional practice in how you help them grow into lifelong learners.

Action 3—Embrace the Problem

Now that we have built a culture of trust, risk-taking and widening perspectives, my students and I are ready to get to work solving big problems. I do this by inviting my students to pick a passion project that aligns with curriculum outcomes. For instance, when I teach my high school students about Canada's history of immigration and settlement, I invite them to consider the experience from a particular perspective of either a newcomer facing the fears and excitement of a new land, government officials who sought to use immigration to achieve larger national goals, or of Indigenous people who experienced the arrival of settlers as a world-changing disruption to their established culture, communities and way of life. With this as my guide, I am able to steer my students' learning on processes that brings out competencies, skills and social-emotional learning. Students learn through a variety of means, including group work, individual student and project-based learning. They learn the content required by the curriculum *and* the literacies, competencies and skills required to be successful in the Fourth Industrial Revolution.

Take Rosalina, for example, who is a traditional high-performing student. Her schooling was mostly teacher lecture–centered, which meant she was trained to write to the test. She wanted to be a doctor, and her first few years of university reinforced her traditional learning style, earning her high marks and acceptance to one of the top medical schools in the world. The medical school faculty used an inquiry-based approach to learning. Just being book smart wasn't going to cut it, and Rosalina found this out the hard way. She ended up struggling mightily her first year and if it wasn't for her support group, she definitely would have left. That's the difference that developing competencies and character traits can have in our students' lives long after they have left our classrooms.

Culture Change Starts With Me

This digital age has placed incredible demands on what and how students learn, which has profound implications for both teachers and teaching. In addition to continuously updating our knowledge of the subjects we teach, teachers are expected to work with multicultural classes, integrate students with special needs, be 'assessment literate,' work and plan in teams, assume some leadership roles and provide professional advice to parents, and don't forget volunteering hours for clubs, groups or sports teams. At first many of these challenges seemed onerous, but by employing Dennis Shirley's new imperatives of educational change, I have been able to gather insights from all these different frameworks to pivot my teaching. By looking at best practices in these jurisdictions and what has worked for others, I created my own framework with ongoing research that works with my strengths and weaknesses as a teacher and the localized needs of my students. More importantly, we need to empathize with students to understand their needs and diversities to create the right learning experiences that meet their needs. The complexities of being a student today are incredible, if you think that from the moment they wake up (and even while they sleep) they are bombarded from all sides with things to do, ways to act and people to please, without really having any time to shut down and relax, thinking only about what they want, need and wish for in this life.

As Sir Ken Robinson said "if done right, they (teachers) become an important asset for the community around them. Great schools enrich the entire neighborhood."[6] Creating the right culture is essential to creating a quality school. Culture is an organic, ever-evolving part of any school. There is definitely bad culture and good culture. But I would never say there is a correct culture. Too many factors come into play to decide if the culture is right for a specific school. What you need is a consistent, strong, clear set of values that have the behaviors, systems and practices in place to uphold a positive, growth-minded educational culture.

Your new approach to classroom planning is rooted in the combination of design, holistic education and culture. It's a lot to think about, but go ahead and dive in. You aren't going to get it absolutely right the first time, but that's the wonder of design thinking: You're not expected to. Rather, continue to tinker and you will see improvements, claim small victories and build momentum on the road to developing a great holistic practice.

Notes

1. World Economic Forum (2015) *New Vision for Education: Unlocking the Potential of Technology.*
2. Sarason, Seymour (1993) *The Predictable Failure of Educational Reform: Can We Change Course Before It's Too Late?* San Francisco: Jossey-Bass.
3. Dweck, Carol (2006) *Mindset: The New Psychology of Success.* New York: Ballentine Books.
4. Dweck, Carol (2016, January 13) "What Having a 'Growth Mindset' Actually Means." *Harvard Business Review.* https://hbr.org/2016/01/what-having-a-growth-mindset-actually-means
5. Schleicher, Andreas (2018) *World Class: How to Build a 21st-Century School System.* Paris: OECD Publishing.
6. Schwartz, Katrina (2016, August 15) "Sir Ken Robinson: How to Create a Culture for Valuable Learning." *KQED.* www.kqed.org/mindshift/46055/sir-ken-robinson-how-to-create-a-culture-for-valuable-learning

6

BUILDING COMMUNITY

Some of my best conversations have happened in cars. A few years ago, I was driving to New York City with some colleagues for meetings and also visiting a few schools with interesting and innovative philosophies. New York City is a 12-hour drive from where I live in Canada, giving us lots of time to talk. One of the reasons I became a teacher is because I like interacting with people. I like figuring out what makes people tick, seeing the world from a different perspective and finding out people's stories. This was a chance for me to get to know my co-teachers, which is extremely challenging in the run of a regular school day. When I was in sales and marketing and before that in coaching, it was expected that I'd meet regularly with colleagues and clients for lunch or a coffee and make time for professional networking events in my community. I had the freedom to call people up to chat. I could get in my car and drive around my territory, observing what was going on in the hopes of using that information to create a win-win for my clients and myself. Teachers don't get to do much of that, and that's a problem as we transform our classrooms for the digital age. We miss out on all the sparks, synergies and projects that are organically being created from meeting and chatting with people outside of our area of expertise.

Out in the rest of the world, traditional hierarchical structures are giving way to flat, interconnected networks that accelerate the free flow of people and information. That's how computer networks operate, how global supply chains operate—and it is increasingly how groups of people operate too. Across almost every topic, groups of people are getting together, united by a common purpose and a commitment to access the collective knowledge of the network to achieve their goals. It is networks that rally volunteers during natural disasters. It is networks that put pressure on local and regional governments to enact change. It is a network that propelled the #MeToo movement into starting to address major inequality issues in North America.

Networking has played a large part in my life in helping me make a difference in my community. So I was pretty excited to get some true brainstorming and collaboration time with colleagues on this road trip because I know the power of networks. You can't do anything world-class without help. The conversation flowed from questions regarding how are we going to teach to the whole child, how do we design for competencies and social-emotional learning, what does the scaffolding look like between grade levels for each competency and many other questions.

Around Portland, Maine, a good six hours into the drive, one of my colleagues wondered out loud why education is always the scapegoat answer for every problem the world and our communities face. Why is it only the school's responsibility to fix global warming, the obesity epidemic, Ebola outbreaks, anxiety issues, low self-esteem and the perils of social media while also teaching foundational literacy and numeracy knowledge? We tossed around our thoughts on the role of schools and teachers in helping to address bigger societal issues. Where has the village gone? How do we bring that incredibly important component back to education? The digital age has made us the most connected, yet we often don't know our neighbors and are not able to leverage these wireless communities into supporting local public education.

If I'm being honest, teaching as a profession is a very isolating existence. It's like any leadership role; it can be lonely even in a crowd. A regular school day begins with my arrival, a quick 'hello' to colleagues in the hall and then it's into my classroom to get ready for first period. There's not a lot of prep time between classes, so what spare time I do have I usually spend getting ready for my next class, making notes about the one I just finished or trying to speak to as many students as I can to check in and continue to build relationships. After school, I may be involved in an extracurricular activity or providing extra help to a student, conferencing with a parent or following up on all the email and phone calls I received while I was teaching that day. Then it's home, greet my wife and my children, have dinner, complete the nighttime routine and then settle in at the kitchen table for an evening of formative assessment, marking or planning. Every part of my workday is scheduled, leaving me not much time to build a network that can help my students' learning as well as push me professionally. And I'm one of the lucky ones. I have an existing network that is quite diversified because of my eclectic background, and I have parents and in-laws that have broad business networks of their own. A friend of mine calls me Forrest Gump, because she says I always seem to know the right person at the right time to make stuff happen.

Since we know how beneficial networking is for student learning and professional development, why don't teachers and leaders push to develop strong community networks, intrasystem networks and global networks? Is it the fact that we are so isolated? Have we been burned too often by people coming in with their own agendas that don't meet the learning outcomes we have designed for students? Is it a lack of collaboration time between the teacher and the community collaborator to prepare and design for the class? Is it the fear of letting helicopter parents enter the classroom? Is it that teachers don't want to be perceived as inept by asking their network for help and showing vulnerability?

Karey Killian in Milton Area School District was introduced to Twitter a few years ago. Her network has expanded to thousands of educators, leaders, policymakers and authors that offer encouragement along with great ideas to provide meaningful opportunities for learning. It's important to her that when her students use an internet search engine to search for her name, they find an example of a role model who posts positive comments while building a community of learning. She states that

> it's important for them to understand how much their written messages impacts the lives of others. My goal is to be the light that encourages others to be their best. Admissions offices and prospective employers will be looking for qualities that help produce the best team players with innovative ideas.

She wants her students and staff to benefit from the application of ideas, shared by innovative leaders around the world. Using social media, she attempts to create the same kinds of learning spaces online that she has created to learn and grow as a professional.

We all have strengths and weaknesses as teachers. Creating a true professional learning community between our school colleagues and between schools within our jurisdiction is key to close the gaps in our professional development and to benefit all our students. Imagine if teachers had an easily navigable database of their peers that they could access for expertise in set design, storytelling 101, 3D printing, coaching creativity and so forth. Peer-to-peer networks to help us scale best practices and enhance our professional practice, with no judgment or fear of reprisal, would benefit everyone involved. Starting with leveraging our best asset in each school, our natural resources—the teachers—would be a great step forward in starting to crowdsource for a successful community of learners.

As teachers, we are preparing our students to operate within this networked world by teaching them the skills, competencies and literacies regarded as necessary for the Fourth Industrial Revolution. While we may be able to create a collaborative environment within our classrooms, we will not be able to claim success until we reach out and connect our classrooms to the community networks that are operating just beyond our school doors, locally and globally.

Local Schools Need Local Networks

Most teachers get this. So too do local school leaders, parents, businesspeople, community volunteers and nonprofit directors. Everyone would like to help; few know how to start, and most don't have the time to try and figure out how. Stephen Ritz does. On the road trip to New York City, my co-teachers and I visited him and got a master class on community building 101. Stephen is a teacher at Community School 55 in the Bronx, one of the poorest areas of the United States. Most children at his school don't eat a vegetable a day, let alone be able to identify most of them. He had an epiphany when he witnessed his students discover a massive number of daffodils secretly growing in the school. Not knowing anything really about science or agriculture, Stephen knew he needed the community and experts to figure out how to use plants in an urban concrete setting to keep this excitement going. And so began the Green Bronx Machine. Stephen is the type of teacher who, when you meet him for the first time, it's as if you've met the best friend you didn't know existed. A larger than life personality with a magnetic charisma and bountiful energy, he has many fans out there, from Oprah to Richard Branson. Imagine Tigger from *Winnie the Pooh* standing over six feet tall and wearing a large 'cheesehead' hat (his trademark). What Stephen understands is that excitement and curiosity drives learning. He had contacts in the community and brought them in to help out his school and students. Strong at building relationships and understanding the power that families have in knowing their children, Ritz invited family members as well—many of whom had never entered the school.

Teachers need to realize that parent advocacy is not a threat. Stephen not only understood that, but he also wanted them involved to help make the learning community stronger. He wanted parents cooking with vegetables at home, planting urban gardens and sharing their successes. Healthy students mean productive students, and having the parents around gave him better insights on how to motivate students. Don't get me wrong—there are many helicopter parents are out there, but teachers can display their professionalism by extending a hand to get the parents' expertise in knowing their child. This will help to build connections and relationships with the student. Collaboration is key.

Stephen Ritz was able to do this and created a community that is now leading a movement all over the world. When you walk into his school, you are in awe of what he has been able to accomplish. My only fear was what happens when he leaves this school? Will Green Bronx Machine die? In this special case, I don't think so, because like he says he doesn't grow plants, he grows people, and he has many people playing large roles now in the ongoing success of this program. But in many other places around the world, strong innovation from one specific teacher often stops once they move schools because they bring the network of the community of learners with them. How do we scale this charismatic community developer that is Stephen Ritz to benefit every teacher, every classroom and every student?

Building relationships is not easy. As a teacher, many elements will impact the paradigms of each student in your class from local politics, national politics, religion, sex, refugees, immigrants, local and global issues and so forth. These forces outside our classrooms that play a large part in forming a child at home, with friends, in sports, at work and so on can conflict with the views of your school or education system. In my experience, that interplay between teachers and students is important in building the right community of learning.

Leah Juelke teaches refugees and immigrant English learners in North Dakota. Her students come from 20 different countries. Developing a classroom culture of respect and positivity can be difficult when students come from such a wide diversity of backgrounds, but Leah is strategic about how she ensures that all of her students feel safe and supported and have a collective motivation to learn. The culture that Leah has developed in her classes has allowed her students to produce award-winning writing. Each year her students produce a collection of short stories and essays that tells how they came to the United States, titled *Journey to America: Narrative Short Stories*. Her class culture is based on respect and humanity, building a community of learners starting with her classroom and spreading to her community.

Practice plays a big part in the culture that we create in our school. Are you willing to work with colleagues, to accept and give constructive feedback, to be self-reflective and to welcome parents into a conversation, your classrooms and your practice? Doing this will help develop the right culture for your practice to flourish. More importantly, developing cordial professional relationships with other members of your school community—colleagues, administrators, parents and students—will increase your confidence in your decision-making leadership abilities. For this type of professional development to happen, you need to have the right behaviors, processes and practices in place to support a growth mindset with no fear of reprisal, mockery or disapproval.

Josh Schachter is one of those teachers able to develop community and networks. However, when he moved schools, he realized that the community he had built at his old school wasn't sustainable because he was the primary networker. Removing him as the main hub of the network meant that it fell apart quickly. In response, he founded Community Share, an online network that connects "the skills and experiences of passionate community partners—professionals, community leaders, organizations and businesses—in the greater Tucson region with the goals and needs of educators in schools and informal learning environments."[1] Teachers can look for different skills and content expertise online and then connect those experts with the students in their classrooms. Community Share is aggressively local, which means all the community partners listed on the site are able to visit classrooms around the city. Josh was inspired to create the network as a way to help connect other teachers with his network in a more organized, self-directed manner.

Creating an online network like Josh's to leverage local expertise and experiences for students can be extremely powerful. For teachers, the network can also provide professional development experiences to enable teachers to update and expand their content-specific expertise. Imagine an English teacher spending time with a local authors' circle, a math teacher shadowing a machine learning specialist at a local company, or a science teacher working alongside the director of a local watershed research center. By leaning on community expertise, we can continue to grow our professional practice using local examples that are relevant to our students.

Most importantly, Community Share is teacher-directed and student-focused. Schools and individual teachers receive a lot of invitations and queries from outside organizations and individuals that want to offer their services and share their knowledge with schoolchildren. This is wonderful, but it can also be problematic. Professional teachers put a lot of thought into the learning arc of their classes. Whether it is over a semester or a full school year, we work hard to ensure our students are continuously progressing on their learning journey. While we are appreciative of all the offers we receive from outside our school walls, it can oftentimes be difficult to determine how best to utilize what the person or group is offering. Community Share solves that problem by handing control to the teacher. It's like Match.com for teachers trying to find the right expert for the right time in their class. They can go through all the opportunities and select who could bring the most benefit to their students, and when.

Stephen Ritz, Leah Juelke and Josh Schachter have developed successful school networks by making use of three important levers: connectors, mentors and transparency.

Connectors: Within our communities we all have connectors, people who can move across different disciplines to make things happen.

They are entrenched in our communities, they know everybody and they can connect you with the people you need to make projects see the light of day. They can find funders, expertise and spaces to make things work. Teachers are getting more adept at connecting. They are active not only in their local communities but also globally, via social media. They leverage parents, grandparents, nonprofits, health care practitioners and businesses to build solid win-win relationships where everyone benefits from the experience. They understand the strength of a network that continuously pays it forward.

Mentors: Finding mentors in the community is another way for the community to play an active part in everybody taking responsibility for our children's education. Mentors can be for students, teachers and principals. Bringing outside community into the schools and schools into the community will enhance agency and show students that their schools are not only learning institutions but key institutions in community building and developing community solutions. Stephen was able to do this through sheer force of charisma and unrelenting dedication to creating a healthier Bronx. Josh built a tool, as a connector, to scale his network of mentors for all teachers to benefit.

Transparency: Building trust is key, and this starts with two-way communication and understanding the power of transparency. By bringing in mentors, parents and community members into the school to help develop students, teachers are also combatting the perception that schools have not evolved. Fixing this one issue for a teacher, for a school, for an education system is one of the foremost pressing issues in education. Why? Because as long as mistrust simmers in your community, you will not get the most out of your education. A school is only as strong as the civic society that it exists within. If culture and values are ill-defined, the school cannot solve or address all the issues. Furthermore, if there is a mistrust between parents and school staff, especially teachers, it will trickle down to the students and the classroom.

Putting the Day on Display

Teachers are great at promoting their students' work: Where many fail is in promoting their own work to others. There is something deep within our professional culture that frowns on teachers stepping up and out. We prefer to keep to the sidelines and let our students have the spotlight. Sadly, that doesn't work very well in a network. The private has become public, and that means teachers need to start talking about and showing their professional accomplishments. This is all about informing for transparency and unity and for rallying the community of learning.

Teachers need to show their work for three important reasons:

- To inform the network so it can support the learning in the classroom;
- To reframe the narrative that the school system is failing our students;
- To become part of the global network of teachers seeking to elevate learning for their students.

Leveraging for the betterment of students needs to start with teachers because we are in charge of the learning process. We know when to use what pedagogy, when to personalize and when to teach to the group. By trusting teachers as professionals and giving them access to community expertise, our students will have quicker development at a deeper level. However, teachers must earn that trust and continue to work to keep that trust. It's ongoing work to build and maintain trust, but that's what creates authentic learning experiences that can push student curiosity.

History is full of examples where the impossible was documented and viewed and informed the world. This not only inspires but also gives permission to challenge the paradigm. By showcasing his program, Stephen Ritz has been able to not only develop his students holistically but also to pave the way for many more around the world in quite similar circumstance to adopt parts of his program. Stephen is connected globally with many other teachers who are part of the Teach Sustainable Development Goals movement (#TeachSDGs), which is helping students to implement local solutions for the United Nations–targeted goals for a sustainable planet. Without showcasing what they and their students do, teachers wouldn't have the understanding of how to connect their worlds to develop global citizenship, collaboration, creativity and communication skills. What these connectors have realized is that competencies development absolutely needs a local and global network.

Competencies Need a Global Community

Leveraging the learning ecosystem to benefit all students is key for developing the pillars in each child, creating the right culture and personalizing their education. Teachers can use networks, both online and in person for the greater good, exponentially pushing social capital in our schools. But first we have to learn how to use it ourselves. Again, this is an opportunity to rethink professional development to help teachers understand how to build community networks because networking between our society's different elements—businesses, nonprofits, government, volunteers, seniors and parents—could definitely help bridge the education gap for many communities. It could also help address other issues in our communities. For instance, my home province of New Brunswick has one of the oldest populations in Canada. We have a growing population of seniors looking for creative ways to stay active and connected in their communities. This is important for geriatric health: Social isolation can often lead to serious health issues. Imagine being able to leverage New Brunswick's active seniors to support learning in local schools. Other examples of this type of intergenerational learning have proven successful at supporting the development of social-emotional learning and other competencies and skills.

In Germany, schools have created strong networks with the trades guilds to encourage students to consider a career in the trades as a way to address the country's labor shortage. This is another example of using networks to address two societal challenges: matching students who are unlikely to attend university with jobs in the trades. Furthermore, it recognizes something that most teachers don't understand or, worse, they choose to ignore: Networks are extremely important for furthering one's path in life in all aspects. If you have the right network, you can reach out for the help you need, whether it is searching for a job, advancing your career or advocating for a cause close to your heart.

When these networks of community are fully integrated across multiple jurisdictions around the world, you can do incredible things to enhance student learning. Take for example Koen Timmers, my friend and co-author of *Teaching in the Fourth Industrial Revolution: Standing on the Precipice*. Koen is a teacher in Belgium who develops large-scale worldwide projects that break down cultural barriers and open up communication to solve world issues. During the Climate

Action Project, he had students from over 80 countries participate in Skype sessions to partner up, collaborate and showcase their solutions for combatting climate change in their local settings. Koen, who is a very active board member and an ambassador for the #TeachSDGs, was able to connect his whole network on social media to further enhance the learning of each student in all of those classrooms around the world.

The power of strong communities of learning locally and globally for every child in every school is one of the challenges that all teachers must address in today's digital age. Otherwise, the social class inequity gap will continue to grow in this disruptive age, because it is not only what you know and what you can do with that learning, but who can help you showcase that knowledge and those competencies.

Note

1. Community Share (2019) "Our Vision and Story." www.communityshare. us/what-is-comshare/

7

TECHNOLOGY INTEGRATION

I am a tech guy. When I go to an education conference, I gravitate to the cool new tech section, happily donning the virtual reality goggles or playing around with an artificial intelligence (AI) game. The coolest by far was controlling a drone with my brain waves, like my childhood dream of becoming a Jedi. At home, just like the rest of us, my smartphone is always close by. Texting has become my main form of communication with friends, and because I am horrible at sitting still, I'll aimlessly flip around the internet, checking out memes, links and social media comments while I'm waiting to pick up my daughters from day care, sitting in the waiting room of my doctor's office or before heading off to bed. That's how most of us live these days, surrounded and enabled by technology, where shutting down is hard.

It certainly is the reality for my students. They've got the world in their pocket, and for better or worse, it's not going anywhere. In fact, the pervasiveness of digital technologies is likely to accelerate over the next decade, particularly in the fields of artificial intelligence and its companion, machine learning. When we listen to experts talk about the Fourth Industrial Revolution, technological change sits at the heart of that transformation. As the World Economic Forum's Klaus Schwab describes it, "we are evolving into a society in which physical, digital and biological systems intermingle and fuse together."[1] Meanwhile, back in the average classroom we're debating whether to let students have access to the calculator apps on their phones. We have some serious decisions to make about when and how technologies are used for student learning. There are certainly some great advantages and there are certainly some serious pitfalls as we fuse the real lives of our students and the learning arcs to develop a holistic education for our students.

I believe many technologies have the capacity to change pedagogical practice, enhance learning and create new cognitive pathways—or simply to be overpriced, cool gadgets. It's our job as teachers to critically assess how and when to use technology in our professional practice. This is what we need to ask ourselves: How do I want to change the learning in my classroom? Based on our answer, which will be rooted in our classroom culture and professional expertise, we can then identify the right mix of technologies to enhance our students' learning. Sadly, that's not what most of us are doing right now. Instead we are presented with a new piece of technology and we try and figure out how to use it in the classroom. It is a subtle but critical difference. We often do not get to choose what tech arrives in our rooms; it is thrust upon us and might not fit what we need. Sometimes we find very interesting deep pathways to fundamental change, but most other times it is a flashy gimmick that soon fades. One thing is always true: It is not the tool but rather how it is used that makes the difference between a gimmick and a transformational learning experience.

Technology integration in education can be a polarizing debate in staff rooms and policy offices around the world. Some believe it is the savior of education, while others believe that it will lead to certain doom. Extreme views on one side argue for more technology in the classroom, including using artificial intelligence and robotics to replace teachers. The other side argues technology should not be allowed because it diminishes the amount of brain power one needs to participate in school, and thus brains will atrophy.

The truth, as usual, can be found somewhere in the middle. Our job as teachers is to work with the larger school community to choose both the appropriate hardware and software and the appropriate ethical guidelines to proceed in a way that aligns with our school and community values. Policymaking is playing catch-up in this area. Most schools and political leaders don't know where to start when it comes to technology policy. What outcomes do we seek? What kind of professional development do teachers need to teach it effectively? How can technology support the larger goals of our education system?

How might technology undermine it? These are some of the questions that we have not stopped to ask in education.

Not so long ago, technology advocates talked about how wonderful it was going to be when students could learn anything, anytime, anywhere. I freely admit that I am guilty of using this slogan in the past. It excites me when students can review a point that I covered in class when they get home, reach out to experts around the world, crowdsource information and access topics pertinent to them. It is absolutely heartwarming when students use assistive technology to overcome struggles around sight, hearing and gross and fine motor skills. However, experience shows us that learning in these new ways, where opportunity, stimulus overload and lack of structure from many channels are normal, needs a strong foundation of knowledge, skills and competencies. This critical foundation is developed throughout your schooling when a holistic approach pushes competencies and social-emotional learning as well as curriculum content. Otherwise, students are bogged down with the amount of content out there without knowing where to start, how to decipher or utilize what's in front of them. As you progress throughout the scaffolding of a holistic education, you become more and more independent and would be able to take advantage of technology's strengths. I still believe in technology's potential to help our students grow into lifelong learners, but it's not all rosy and bright. New and emerging technologies are having a mixture of effects on our students, our classrooms and our teaching profession, and it is our task to discern power from gimmick and use wisdom to know why, when, what, where and how to use technology for learning.

Take Khan Academy, which has done a fantastic job of combining videos with automated assessment software and a little bit of AI to track the progress of students and ask carefully timed review questions. This allows students to proceed at their own pace, which is a great way to supplement classroom work or provide classes in places that may not have a vast set of offerings to proceed with curriculum outcomes for knowledge and some skills. There are fantastic opportunities to help personalize the learning of many different students while simultaneously bringing a certain level of equity and consistency by combining delivery of content through video and using available AI algorithms to help direct assessment for and of learning. For as much power as these tools hold, they also represent a seriously dangerous slippery slope away from a great resource for the classroom teachers for which they were intended and toward the dark side—that teachers can be replaced by an automated system.

It is completely realistic that an education system that believes teaching is an occupation would absolutely attempt replacing and automating teachers. It has in fact been tried with much pomp and circumstance as the way of the future, with disastrous effect. Policymakers, for-profit schools, and for-profit EdTech companies touted this vision as a fantastic step forward, using all of the buzzwords. They even provided inspirational stories about outlier students who experienced success in these environments. However, in reality, it was a horrible experiment with our youth and it is scary to think it might be used again. A private school system was set up with large rooms and 300 students in individual cubicles, which looked very similar to a call center. Each student sat at a computer, and the room was patrolled by more of a security officer than a teacher. Students could choose what class to take at what time in the day and could follow at their own pace. It sounded very progressive and "personalized." However, everyone is on the identical sequence of learning inside that class, which makes it easily standardized for curriculum content. They use the jargon of personalized learning, but yet it was more robotic and totally disregarded all the other aspects of the pillars of learning holistically, which would have really personalized the learning. Certainly, there are some unfortunate and unique situations where such an education is useful, but I do not believe it is a viable solution for the masses. Where are the conversations between students, the synergy of ideas during a brainstorm, the critical thinking of a debate when a student's point of view is challenged, or the comradery of solving a real problem for real people with your fellow students?

The same buzzwords of choice, autonomy and pace for personalized learning can leverage technology to make connections, reach out into the world and create. Jack (not his real name), a history student wanting to do medicine, used technology to reach out to medical experts and anthropologists to see how surgery evolved through wars. Because of the technology of 3D printing, this student could 3D print a skull, fill it with butter (a brain analogue) and actually perform a mock surgery for his peers, explaining the evolution and why it would have been unethical to do so in peacetime, or any time. Given the opportunity, technology can personalize learning by allowing a multitude of paths that allow students to reach out into the world, create something interesting and push it back out to the world. When you have access to technology such as video, cameras, the internet, green screen, 3D printing and virtual reality, you are able to showcase your learning in a different way. This means that the pedagogical approach can shift. Students and teachers alike can become creators.

With great pedagogical practice, technology can be transformative. Student with selective mutism are able to have a voice via multiple apps; a dyslexia font brings equity to students who feel marginalized; students with anxiety are able to self-regulate with a heart monitor or a mindfulness app; glasses help autistic children recognize social cues; multiple mediums open up the possibilities for students to showcase their learning; instant formative feedback machines for teachers enable speech to text to sticker, saving countless hours of marking, finally giving student feedback in a time-sensitive manner; social media gives students the ability to advocate for issues locally in a global spectrum; the student has the ability to also self-reflect on the process, giving teachers insight into not just the product but also the scaffolding. The opportunities are great as long as pedagogical practice is strong.

Schools need to be places that help students develop healthy social media habits, critically assess the role technology will play in their careers and lives, and determine how technology can help solve local and global problems. Teachers must become both advocates and moral guides for our students and their families as schools and education systems seek to determine how best to integrate technology so it may help rather than hinder our development.

Technology and Our Students

Our students are growing up in a different world from that in which we grew up. It is a much more invasive, connected and critical place. While teens have been doing dumb and immature things for generations, this is the first generation that may never be allowed to forget their youthful mistakes. I know I've got stuff in my past best forgotten, and because I came of age before mobile and digital technologies, it is forgotten. Not so for my students. Now, technology pervades all aspects of a student's life, 24 hours a day, 7 days a week, 365 days a year. Mistakes go viral and are recorded for anyone to search, long after they should have been forgotten.

Smartphones are pervasive, which means there is no separation of home and school. It all melds together. No longer are there dead times and spaces where students can be alone and chill out. Students have embraced wireless technologies without fully understanding how to use them. And why would they? It's not like adults are modeling the best examples. We are all terrible at filtering the steady stream of information that flows through our lives. Every experience, every emotion, every day must be captured and shared—often as it is happening—with friends and strangers alike on social media. Every time that phone dings or vibrates, we are looking for that boost of recognition—and when it doesn't come, we worry that we've offended the wrong person, said something stupid or simply lost the attention of the crowd.

As a teacher, I know there is direct correlation between higher anxiety, stress and bullying issues and the use of technology 24/7. As bad as bullying and hazing was in the past, at least there was an escape at home. Now the bullying can happen anytime, anyplace with a whole school participating or viewing, and it appears that our girls are particularly vulnerable. I don't need a research paper to tell me that this is happening. I see it every day. Our students have a fear of being trolled all the time, so they feel the need to be perfect and to showcase this perfection to the world. This behavior is the exact opposite of what needs to be taught in the 21st-century classroom—build trust, collaborate with your peers, learn to adapt and lead with empathy. These are the core competencies and character traits we are told employers value. How do we bridge the gap between our students' reality and the education they'll need in the Fourth Industrial Revolution?

We are not the only ones unsure of what to do next. Parents need an education about youth and social media. When should children be allowed to use social media? Which platforms? Should they set time limits? How do they monitor their children's activities? For instance, sneaking around on social media can carry far greater ramifications than sneaking home after curfew. I've known students to have two, three and even four sets of social media accounts, the one created with and for their parents and a few that their parents and even friends don't know exist. These students are living multiple lives, which increases both their isolation and their exposure to high-risk activities and people.

At the same time, I have witnessed my students use wireless technologies and social media to deepen their connection to causes and people all over the world, to independently pursue knowledge on topics of interest to them and to boldly reach out to experts to ask questions about the world. For instance, Katie witnessed an acquaintance being bullied. She leveraged connectivity that social media provides. Between the end of day on a Thursday and Friday morning, she connected with the school administration, received permission to host a rally in the gymnasium and let it be known through the whole school population and to the general public. Before the national anthem was sung the next day, there were over 300 students, parents and general public in the gym making signs and T-shirts in support of the victim.

This is the only world our students have ever known: a hyperconnected, information-saturated frontier with few rules and a multitude of choices. It's our responsibility as teachers to show them how to begin to build a new society upon this digital foundation.

Technology and Our Classrooms

When we consider the World Economic Forum's three pillars of education in the Fourth Industrial Revolution, digital literacy is a single subhead within the larger category of "literacies." But that infers technology is just a subject, and that's not correct. It's a tool, which means we need to determine how and where to use multiple technologies across all elements of our professional practice.

For me, the issue of technologies in the classroom can be broken out into three primary questions:

- How do we teach students to think about how they use technology (critical thinking)?

- How do we determine when and where to use technology to enhance student learning (teaching tools)?
- How do I protect my students' privacy when using collaborative and cloud-based technology (professional ethics)?

Critical thinking: Social media has polarized public debate and divided us up into groups with narrow self-interest. This hardening of opinion is extremely dangerous, and I fear if it is left unchecked it could leave us with a generation of self-interested, resentful citizens incapable of solving complex challenges in their personal lives or in the world at large. What is our role as classroom teachers in trying to bring different perspectives to the debate? Should students be able to understand something that is posted, how it impacts their person and those around them? Should they be able to spot fake news and where it comes from? What are other perspectives? Will this give students the ability to look at a post and news source and comment through multiple lenses and perspectives?

Teaching tools: While there is a constant flow of new and interesting technologies on the market every day that may be very useful for the rest of the world, with limited time and budgets we need to be judicial in our decisions around technology. I love technology and I love being on the edge of innovation. Yet we don't have many school systems around the world that are actually connecting and in partnerships with the academics and the private world to lead research and development for education. How many teachers come up with innovative ideas and would love to validate them on a larger scale but cannot, either because the purse strings are controlled at the top or they lack the resources to do so based on their location? So, teachers gravitate to what is free, which isn't always what is best or ethical. Action-based research, feedback, stories and evidence need to be assessed to better understand the impact of technology integration on children, teenagers and young adults. When should they be getting hardware? What type of hardware? What type of software? What about video games? If we had a properly funded research and development department, it could be designed by the teacher leading the software and support team to develop what is truly needed for a strong holistic public education system that benefits all of society.

Is the technology in and of itself sufficient to warrant technology integration? Is the technology making a real change in the cognitive tasks of students? Consider the issue of coding and computer science in the classroom, which has gone through a few iterations over the past four decades. These days teachers are debating whether students can learn other disciplines via coding. While I am excited about the flexibility of a teacher to allow students an opportunity to demonstrate their learning with some sample of code, I am not convinced that coding teaches more math or language or enhances the study of civics, except for those students who simply love to code. I am convinced that it does bring out some competencies and social-emotional learning. However, coding shouldn't be a priority in every subject area.

For me, one of the most exciting areas of growth in technology for learning is assistive technology. For instance, improved speech-to-text functions allow students with limited fine motor skills to record their thoughts, ideas and responses in a timely manner without additional adult resources. There are some exciting examples of how technology can be used to develop communication, collaboration, critical thinking, creativity, citizenship and character. I am also excited about the power of video to enhance learning. In my classroom, we regularly use free videoconferencing software to speak with both students and subject matter experts in different countries to discuss Sustainable Development Goals (SDG's), how they can play a part in the solution and how they can partner up to collaborate. As an example, one student in my World Issues class is working with an optometrist and students from an African country to 3D-print eyeglass frames. Often the post-discussion prompts students to self-reflect about their role in solving these global challenges, which builds understanding and empathy as well as empowerment and courage. Reaching out into the world is terribly valuable for teachers' professional development too, because making connections with peers is a practical step toward a more realistic worldview and a tangible step toward true global citizenship.

Professional ethics: There are strict ethical guidelines around data collection and archiving in the research world. The data must have a very specific use, researchers may only collect the data needed to complete their work and this data must be stored in a secure location for a set period of time before being deleted. How do we collect, store and dispose of all the data being produced by students and teachers as part of daily classroom activities? Few if any schools have thought about this potentially thorny issue.

For instance, let's think about how teachers use video in classrooms. There's videoconferencing software to connect students with people around the world, self-reflection video journals, video as part of student presentations and students viewing streaming services such as YouTube and Vimeo. That's four different uses of video. To access those video services, teachers depend on cloud-based software and free social media platforms—all of which require students to sign in. That means those free online services now have personal information and can track whoever signed in. What responsibility do teachers have to protect students' identities and their work? Is that even possible?

Furthermore, the same technology can be used to track teacher performance and the goings-on in the classroom. What will happen if school systems start posting cameras in the classroom, analyzing every second, every word, every interaction? Does that benefit the teacher's or student's development? You could argue that within a professional development week, it would be highly beneficial to get peer review and be able to self-reflect after seeing yourself in action. But if it was all the time, I fear that it would have more to do with policymakers wanting to have documentation to assert control.

Teachers cannot on the one hand stand in front of students and profess to be experts in digital literacy and online behavior, if on the other hand they are not critically assessing their classrooms' cyber-risk and determining ways to improve their cyber-awareness.

Moving Forward With Intent

Technology has the capacity to play a role in helping education move forward or leading to its demise. It is the attitudes, philosophies and actions of the humans that will determine where we go. We will choose the future that we deserve, therefore we must be very conscious and conscientious about how we proceed.

Students will need strategies to help them develop their digital literacy to understand how their digital footprint is formed, how to behave online and how to integrate technology into their lives to help them become collaborators, creators, innovators and self-sufficient adults living and working in the Fourth Industrial Revolution. Teachers need to be their community's leaders so that we may all succeed in a digital age.

Note

1. Schwab, Klaus (2016) *The Fourth Industrial Revolution*. New York: Crown Business.

8

ASSESSMENTS AND THE IMPACT ON LEARNING CULTURE

About a decade ago I went from being a couch potato to an Ironman athlete in 18 months. I was an elite athlete growing up, playing multiple team sports, but in university a concussion sidelined me for good. When I lost the ability to play, I lost myself. I lazed around, ate a lot of junk food and generally felt sorry for myself. It continued through my career in sales and it wasn't until I decided to become a teacher that I started to change. I had found a purpose in life and with it, my old competitive spirit returned. I threw myself into training, setting a goal to go from 270 pounds down to 185 pounds in time for my first Ironman event and, like most people on weight loss programs, I became obsessed with numbers. I needed to quantify everything.

An Ironman is a 2.4-mile swim, a 112-mile bike ride and a 26.2-mile run. I had experience running, but I hadn't swum since I was a kid, I didn't cycle and my diet was a mess. In an Ironman, understanding and succeeding with nutrition during training and the day of the race is essential. You can do every athletic move perfectly, but if you screw up your hydration and nutrition you won't finish. With four disciplines to plan for, monitor and analyze, my life revolved around data collection and analysis. I counted and measured everything, and for a period of time it really helped me improve my performance. I would see a big improvement for a few weeks and then I'd plateau, which was frustrating because I was putting in a tremendous effort but not seeing much improvement.

This is typical of any big endeavor, and student learning is no different. Quantitative data collection and analysis can provide us with great feedback on our teaching and help chart a student's progress, but they alone cannot get us to the finish line. You might realize that a certain content, skill, or strategy that you taught only has a 25 percent success rate on a formative or summative evaluation for every student. With a few changes in pedagogical approach, you might be able to bring it up to 75 percent, but to reach that final 25 percent you need to dig into the qualitative data, the personal stories behind the numbers.

Looking over my four years of Ironman data, I can point out exactly where I made systematic improvements from using quantitative data and where the jump in improvements from stale weeks came from me listening to the small cues my body was sending me. That qualitative data told me the everyday story of my numbers, which included how I felt, what techniques I was using and what was going on around me at that point in time. If I hadn't embraced a holistic approach to my assessment, I would have missed important cues that could have derailed me before I even reached the starting line. Oftentimes, listening to the qualitative data unleashed a dramatic improvement in one area of my training that gave me the scaffold to build strategies to improve in another. Who'd have thought an Ironman competition could prepare me for student assessments?

Learning to Measure What Matters

There is a big push these days to quantify everything in education and in every other sector. This is done to be able to categorize and pinpoint exactly where a child is in their learning journey. Numbers are easy to understand: It's easier to just accept and try to improve on a number. However, many of the competencies, skills, character traits and social-emotional learning we should be teaching are not easily measured because they are humanistic elements. Some report cards already have numbers associated with leadership or grit. But, what does a 89 percent in communication or a 42 percent in creativity really mean? Competencies are always evolving and may present differently depending on the subject matter. It certainly isn't as simple as marking a test. It requires more nuanced means of assessment and should never just be a number. And the truth is, for content and skills assessment, most teachers struggle with putting a number because it disregards the evolution of the child and the stories behind the learning. Furthermore, we have yet to determine how to adequately assess competencies and social-emotional learning, the core of Fourth Industrial Revolution learning. Self-reflection and input from many sources are key parts to this growth process. How and why do we sum that up with a number? No statistical report will ever be able to point us to full answers. In any complex system, numbers tell only half the story. Companies that have embraced big data have also hired people—specialists—who can interpret the data and recommend next steps. These analysts look at big data trends, but they must dig deeper when they see fluctuations to get the stories behind the statistics. In education, those experts are already in the system—they are us, the teachers.

Then how do we assess leadership in our students? Should we look at strengths and understand when to help them out earlier? Would boys benefit from play-based study to direct their innate curiosity toward school subjects? Would this get more boys interested in stepping into academic leadership? Would girls benefit from girls-only STEM exercises in middle school to showcase their strengths in the field? The middle school years seem to be the time they lose their belief in their abilities.

Don't get me wrong. Quantitative data certainly has its place, but it needs to be combined with qualitative data at all times. Every case is unique and we need to realize that students will never develop further than a certain point without specific attention to each of them based on their zone of proximal development. Every part of the education system is a constant balancing act. It is no different in assessment.

Data in the Classroom

In my high school history class, I used the following qualitative assessment system to support quantitative data. If you look at any paper I grade, it doesn't matter if it's the 'top' student or the 'lowest' student when it comes to curriculum outcome knowledge; they will both have the same amount of written feedback at the start of the year. It usually is in the style of questions, because nothing in history is the exact truth, it always has multiple perspectives. This gives me the opportunity to further develop my high flyers. What I am doing with them is developing resiliency to obstacles from curriculum content, which for the most part they have never had because of their ability to memorize. For them, it's all about knowing where they are in terms of character and social-emotional learning and pushing those paradigms with this assignment. For the ones who struggle, they realize that everyone has the same amount of growth when they see that everyone has the same amount of questions in feedback. The complexities of the questions differ between the different students, but the amount on the page is the same no matter what. This also helps in the creation of an open culture.

You can see quite clearly a design thinking process linked with the development of culture and trying to hit multiple pillars of a holistic learning experience. Using quantitative data to see where the class might have missed something within the curriculum content outcomes, I can approach my next lesson or do remedial work with a smaller group. But in terms of a holistic learning experience, it's about concentrating on the individuals in front of me. Add to this a self-reflection piece that helps the student start to understand where they stand in how they learn and how to become lifelong learners, and you have a way to mix quantitative and qualitative data analysis that is teacher-led and student-focused.

If education is pivoting toward a more holistic approach, we need to understand how that will impact the dynamics of the classroom and how assessment can be done to further develop all pillars. Depending on the subject, it can be quite time-consuming and labor-intensive. Balancing what needs to be assessed and what might not need to be is key. Peter Drucker famously gave us the quote: "what gets measured, gets managed." That is precisely why education systems, school leaders and teachers must carefully plan what they measure. Measure the wrong thing and you will soon have a school system with poor performance or with great measures for only one specific pillar of a holistic learning experience.

Let's consider how we might measure and address education policies' effect on teachers and their ability to teach competencies and social-emotional learning to students. What impact does 'nobody fails' policies have on classroom dynamics with content and skills? What would a longitudinal study tell you about the individual that went up to the next grade level without meriting it? What about the group dynamics? Overall, how does that pan out in society? Are we even capable to answer that question yet?

So what needs to be managed for successful high-performing holistic education systems? Should you measure every pillar and all the elements within a pillar with quantitative data? Should you measure every pillar and all the elements within that pillar with qualitative data? Should you measure every pillar with both exhaustive quantitative and qualitative data? We know that critical feedback at the right time, said the right way, can improve development. Basically, a well-timed comment will be much more effective on competency, social-emotional learning or skills development than a delayed number on a report card with no portfolio, context or story behind it. Does it become about developing the pillars or reporting on the pillars? If we overmandate, through policy, numbers evaluation for competencies and social-emotional learning, the inevitable results will be the production of rubrics and report cards to ensure accountability and for kids to be sorted, never knowing the true stories of our education systems and the children within it.

Taking the Politics OUT of Assessments

After many conversations with my colleagues around the world about assessment, I have discerned three general observations. First, data is often misused for political purposes. Second, there is an overemphasis on collecting data without a corresponding strategy to determine its purpose. Third, one-off or limited data points are often used as excuses to make drastic changes, which can have a negative impact on school culture and learning. Education systems and schools need a better approach to data strategy and management.

There is a divide between how assessments are applied and what it means for individual students, between execution and outcomes. Quantitative-driven policy change often doesn't align with the holistic learner profile that most systems claim to embrace and often emphasize in their major policy documents. Standardized testing can objectively compare students' content knowledge and skill levels across schools if they are written in a way that doesn't advantage a certain part of the school population. It can help identify specific individual or classroom gaps, and when combined with the right pedagogical approach it can help drive their learning. However, like Hattie says "leaders in education need to make sure teachers are shown how to use data to each student's advantage".[1] I would argue that it is true that teachers need a personalized approach to assessment, but that leaders also need to understand how to use that data and not make broad-stroke policies without looking at things more closely to classrooms and individual student stories.

Consider high-stakes standardized testing, which is used in some states to determine teachers' salaries. When used in this manner, teachers bear the full responsibility for student achievement. It is a perspective that fails to recognize whether the system in which the teacher works provides adequate supports to students to ensure they are ready to learn when they step into the teacher's classroom. It's akin to tying doctors' salaries to their patients' health records. George (not his real name) told me the story that in one state, teachers dreaded being assigned a high-performing class because there was little room for growth, which led the administration to question their abilities as a teacher in developing students, which resulted in a decrease in salary. In this cutthroat system, teachers hope for just below average students that they can show improvement with their "hard work" as teachers with a resulting larger pay. It is the system, structures and policy that are affecting education in a very negative way. Teacher pay should not be linked to high-stakes standardized testing. And even if that system is encouraging through policy that teachers will develop competencies and social-emotional learning, the reality is that teachers will feel pressured to teach to the high-stakes standardized test based on content because of the consequences.

In a perfect world, none of the students in our schools would have any issues. Everyone would be a sponge, ready to absorb all knowledge, competencies, skills, social-emotional learning, literacies and character without worrying about all the possible elements influencing the learning process. That's not the reality. It is easy to go for the low-hanging fruit when the complexities of each child's issues can be overwhelming, particularly without adequate support or resources. However, teaching to the test, specifically in a high-stakes standardized testing environment, is problematic in schools that are lacking the appropriate supports. Teachers are able to personalize the learning process they have designed based on all the assessment points. Students can and do showcase learning in different ways. Often it helps to incorporate parents in the learning process by including them in formative assessment, such as student sleeping patterns and asking what the student does in their spare time. Learning happens at any time, both formally or informally. Sitting down with a grandparent as they recount stories of their youth, immersing in another culture through travel, learning how to network and speak with others and helping out at the local food bank; all of these are informal learning opportunities that if addressed with certain open-ended questions for self-reflection can be as strong as any formal learning happening in the classroom.

High-stakes standardized testing has another serious problem: showcasing one element in a specific time, from one specific group. Unless you look over a number of years to compare results over a long period of time, making any dramatic changes over only one result doesn't make any sense. Assessment should be ongoing and fluid using both big, small, quantitative and qualitative data. Yes, it can showcase gaps in learning for that existing cohort, but it is oftentimes done as a one-off and without looking at pre-post data with the same students.

I have realized successful education systems all share similar attributes: Teachers are treated as professionals and the education system has been depoliticized. For the most part, they leave education to the experts. This doesn't mean that society is not consulted and that there is no change. I have seen these systems use data when the time is needed to pivot and leave the small data to the teacher's discretion to improve their students.

When education assessments appear in an election campaign, teachers and students rarely come out the winners in the debate because oftentimes the data is used to misconstrue and manipulate the reality to suit the candidate's or party's larger plan. It usually is specific to one of the literacies or questions why the school system hasn't solved a larger social issue, neither of which ever works as a quick fix. Educational reforms happen over years. Leadership and teachers can monitor results, but oftentimes we won't know how successful we've been until a full cohort of students has passed through. But how many policies have been implemented because of data and then dropped within a year? How many systems change policies every time there's a change in government? If education systems are serious about building a sustainable able-to-change-as-needed education culture, they need to stop nickeling-and-diming education based on the interpretation of only a few numbers from one or two assessments and the analysis of one person. Our students deserve better.

High-performing systems seem to have struck a balance with all the data points, quantitative, qualitative, big and small, able to be collected within classrooms, schools and systems. Foolishly the focus over the last generation has been curriculum content and skills heavy for university or bust. One element I would caution is that some of those high-performing systems on PISA (particularly in science, math and literacies) are teaching to the test, which reinforces that book smarts take precedence over any other kind in our societies. It has created a perception that university education is the pinnacle of postsecondary study. Everything else is perceived to be a lesser path in society. This is not appropriate and directly correlated to the way data has been used in direct contradiction to every talk I have heard from the head of PISA, Andreas Schleicher. The result, I believe, is a growing labor shortage in the skilled trades and a generation of young people pursuing university degrees at great cost and debt, just to turn around and figure out that they don't want to work in those fields. Within a sustainable, growing society, every job has value.

Take for example farming, a sector that is struggling to attract young people. Why don't more students want to be a part of the sector responsible for our food supply, especially when it is taking on dramatic changes involving urban farming, hydroponics and drone crop mapping. Agriculture is an exciting multidisciplinary profession that will always require workers. What about the trades? We need plumbers, carpenters, laborers and electricians. Why can't we have a certain level of schooling that is acceptable for the pillars and then we can find ways to help people use their strengths and be proud of their work? A crane operator can make six figures stepping out of his program—I bet you not too many students know that figure. But they all know how much a doctor or lawyer can make. I'm not talking about reducing education, content, skills, social-emotional learning or competencies development. I'm saying why can't we raise the value of all work?

It's the same as being only 'street smart' or 'book smart.' Who would you want in a pinch? You would want someone who is both. Yet formal schooling at this time really only pushes the book smart, or at least that's what it feels like to students. Meanwhile, teachers are being told that freshmen are struggling in their first year of post-secondary studies. They don't have the 'street smarts' to navigate their new settings. They are lacking the character traits, competencies and social-emotional learning that are required to function successfully in contemporary society. Teachers know how to prep students, but we need administrators and policy leaders to let us. That can't happen if teachers are conditioned to teach to the test and reprimanded if they don't. Standardized testing has shifted the pedagogical practice, resource allotment and leadership/management styles, and we need to rectify this if we hope to properly prepare students for the Fourth Industrial Revolution.

Moving Forward

What does an education system need to assess in order to develop the student in all aspects of life? What does an education system need to assess to help teachers reach every child? What does a school leader need to assess to help the students flourish in all aspects of life? What does a school leader need to assess to help teachers reach students? What does a school leader need to assess to improve his leadership? What does a teacher need to do? In this digital age, this isn't as clear as the change makers, system leaders and politicians want teachers to believe. Changing a system is a constant balancing act because you are dealing with children, who are complex and unique beings.

Discussions regarding what and how we collect data should be ongoing as part of our professional practice. For instance, I believe we should figure out how to assess a student's development in the process of self-reflection and the scaffolding that comes with it. If our goal is to develop lifelong learners, being able to self-reflect teaches students how to filter through all their data points in order to adjust, adapt and accept what life throws at them and learn. This would also serve to convert the assessment process into a collaborative practice between students and teachers. The process could start very simply, with the student and teacher working together to construct the scaffolding necessary to help the student understand how to simplify complex situations. It's a lifelong strategy that can be applied to any form of learning, whether it is learning to play basketball, learning to cook for yourself or achieving great academic success. This is how we will help our students truly master becoming strong, resourceful, capable lifelong learners in any discipline.

Note

1. Brown, Gavin T. L. and John Hattie (2016) https://academia.edu/1964802/ The_benefits_of_regular_standardized_assessment_in_childhood_education_ Guiding_improved_instruction_and_learning

Conclusion

Education globally is on a journey, and the start of this new digital age will be marked as a major historical moment. The world is changing, and for someone who teaches history, reminders are everywhere of what we study. The teaching of history has shifted in the last ten years; it is less about memorizing random dates and facts and more about understanding multiple perspectives, creating a better, well-rounded picture of events that are sculpting our world. The more I teach history, the more I realize that it's not just the event, but every little event combining together. This shift has led me to put most of my emphasis in the classroom on concepts influenced by the University of British Columbia's Peter Seixas, which include cause and consequence, historical perspective, historical significance, continuity and change, primary sources and ethical dimension. If you take any of those elements, you'd be hard-pressed not to conclude that our current era parallels the industrial revolution and the subsequent rise of nationalism and autocratic regimes. With all the disruption, we are getting a new elite and the rest of us are suffering through these massive changes. It is a scary time. In this type of disruption, we need leadership with ethics. We need visionaries. We need thought leaders. We need doers. And we need them now, otherwise we are in danger of losing what is good in our existing systems.

Our public education system is not broken. Does it need to change with the times? Of course. It needs proper support with some pivots to update it for today's world. In these pages I have shared with you my perspective from classroom, schools and education systems from around the world on what those changes need to be. In Chapter 1, we explored what it means to be a teacher at this point in history. In Chapter 2, I championed that teachers are empowered and are leaders as respected professionals, and I challenged the occupational models of teaching that are used in some countries. In Chapter 3, I explored how to create a more robust profession through initial teacher education, supporting the onboarding of new teachers with structures and mentors and ongoing professional development to bring back the calling.

In Chapter 4, I explained how design thinking could be applied in the classroom to create a learning environment for the complexities of the digital age. In Chapter 5, I described how teachers can address all pillars of a holistic personalized education for students by intentionally designing a culture of learning. In Chapter 6, I tackled the inherent isolation of teachers with an invitation to reach out into the wider community to build professional networks. In Chapter 7, I addressed the complexities of technology integration and its impact on learning, and in Chapter 8, I confronted teachers' conflicted feelings toward assessment. Yet none of these reforms and changes will happen if we don't get leadership, policy and implementation in public education right.

Leadership needs to come from teachers, but we need to advocate for more than just our professional roles: We must take a stand and advocate for the soul of education itself. We need to create strong ethical partnerships with other sectors to create the right ecosystem. We need to uphold true teacher standards. We need to embrace ethical and meaningful innovation and supportive technologies that can help our pedagogical practice. We must fight back as we renovate this most important institution and yes, I do put education in the same breath as the judiciary, legislative and executive institutions. If we let education erode and allow it to be taken over by private entities or autocratic regimes that place AI and robotics, not teachers, in front of our children, we will be heading down a dangerous path.

In a world with more and more autocratic rule, how do teachers rise up for the soul of education? We have seen teachers around the world taking a stand and speaking up. We need to support our colleagues around the world in their local fights for learning, for standards, for excellence, for schools, for students.

Leadership is about hope. In education, we tend to only speak about problems. If you always speak about problems and never about the elements that are going great, you are confirming what people may hear and have accepted is the truth about education. The great stories, the great work, the incredible things going on in classrooms around the globe are hardly ever celebrated on the front page of the news or shared on social media. It's always about the problems in education and how to 'fix our failing schools.' Few people actually understand what is going on or what changes have already been introduced. The old industrial-age classroom is already making its way to the history books. Very rarely have I walked into a classroom that looked like the schooling my grandparents would have described.

Great political leadership trusts teachers to develop workable solutions. It can be from the correct policymaking at the right time, school leadership finding funds to make projects happen, school leadership designing a new bell schedule, a new framework or a new learning environment with teachers, or teachers taking action when presented with obstacles. People in education are getting away from the why and what and are getting to the how. But while we are beginning to see change, it is unevenly distributed.

There is still a high degree of inertia in our systems, and to tell you the truth, I don't blame the policymakers and administrators for staying neutral in many situations. At this point in history, there's not a lot of trust in our political classes, and so the civil service and professional educators are wary, worried that if something goes wrong, their political partners will be quick to assign blame. Teachers have seen it around the world: the manipulation and reinterpretation of stories, news or data in service to other agendas that may not have the best interests of students at heart. Over the last three decades the pendulum has swung wildly from school leadership to school administrators, from district leadership to district administrators. This needs to stop. The system needs to be apolitical for it to be sustainable.

Teachers need lawmakers who treat education as seriously as security because in so many ways, education is security. A country that cannot think is just as dangerous as a country that cannot defend itself. When the divide between social classes continues to grow, this is scary. Public education is the foundation of great societies. When you don't value the strengths of each child, when you don't develop each child holistically, when you don't make each child feel significant, when you only offer one way to a decent life, when you disproportion the taxes only to the wealthy, your society will crumble. The bottom line is this: We must design our systems to ensure all students flourish.

Teachers will do that. From our classrooms we will guide the change, and together we'll build a better world for all of us.

Teaching life: This is what we do with passion and commitment, for our students, our communities and our world.

Other Praise for This Book

This book is a wonderful call that inspires teachers to innovate and feel proud of their profession, written by one of the most highly regarded teachers in the world. Clearly and beautifully written, Armand's book uplifts me as a leader of teachers and I am sure it will make every teacher who reads this work feel better about the truly honorable profession to which they dedicate their lives.

—Vicky Colbert, Founder and Director of Fundación
Escuela Nueva, Yidan Prize Laureate for
Educational Development (2017)

One of the most critical tasks of professionals in any field is to make sense of their work and of the challenges of their practice which are messy, which don't have predefined answers. Tackling those problems requires sophisticated knowledge that draws on the self-examined practice of good members of the profession. In this book, Armand Doucet gives us a masterful example of reflective practice. He shares with us the everyday life of a teacher, and from the analysis of aspects of that experience, particularly of the challenges that he faces in practice, he makes sense of why those challenges exist, and draws on the rich knowledge base he has gained as a lifelong learner, curious about his field and about the world, to suggest ways in which the conditions that support the profession of teaching could be reimagined. Anyone interested in understanding the profession of education should read this book.

—Fernando M. Reimers, Ford Foundation Professor of the Practice of International Education and Director of the Global Education Innovation Initiative, Harvard Graduate School of Education

Doucet is a history teacher and he brings himself and his students to the whole wide world. He seems to have cloned himself inside and outside the classroom. He stands alone, and he stands collectively with students and other teachers. He frames choices around design, building things, technology, community and assessment—all woven into a lively learning adventure. In *Teaching Life* he shows how teaching can be a ticket to boundless imagination, and an energizing but focussed romp into learning about oneself and the world. Doucet has written a stimulating and compelling book to act and learn in concert.

—Michael Fullan, O.C., Professor Emeritus, OISE/University of Toronto

This book provides invaluable insights into teaching. Any educator or education program that is working on preparing and developing teachers for today's world would greatly benefit from this book.

—Soulaymane Kachani, Vice Provost for Teaching and Learning, Columbia University

After *Teaching in the Fourth Industrial Revolution*, another amazing book on education, this time for and about teachers, who are changing the world every day in millions of classrooms, by opening young minds for critical thinking, innovation, skills and emotional learning.

Teaching Life is a passionate and engaging story of teaching, as Doucet simply and beautifully says: "Becoming a teacher is more than a career choice; it is for many of us a calling."

It is another must read for anyone interested in championing classroom-focused change. It is a book that raises important questions about education as a new vision about more than simply preparing students for a technologically-advanced world, but also about how education can prepare them to embrace values such as equity, justice, peace and human rights.

It is a book that invites us to think how through education we can "refine and rediscover our common humanity."

—Irina Bokova, Director General
UNESCO (2009–2017)

No revolution is possible without genuine grassroot movement. Unfortunately, education has been, traditionally, a hierarchical, top down system where we haven't been putting enough emphasis on the role of the teachers—listening to them and giving them a voice. Armand Doucet is on a mission to change this. In this insightful, passionate and timely book, he writes that we need visionaries, thought leaders and doers. It is obvious that he is all three.

—Saku Tuominen, Founder of HundrED

Teaching Life is a most welcome contribution to collective efforts to ensure that we are able to realize the promise of Agenda 2030 and of SDG 4 in particular. It is most timely especially when multilateralism and global solidarity is under threat in a context of "widespread economic, social and political unrest and communities are racing to figure out their place in our emerging new world." It is without doubt that teachers, as this book underscores, are central to ensuring that young and old alike are able to navigate an uncertain future with hope and with the requisite skills and competencies to confront challenges but also to take advantage of the opportunities that a new future offers. A future that is more equal and safer, and one in which we value each other and the planet. That any global conversation on the future of education and lifelong learning is incomplete without teacher voices was affirmed at the recent Global Education Meeting in Brussels (December 2018); and that teachers, school leaders, educators and trainers play a vital role in our collective responsibility to prepare future generations.

—Jordan Naidoo, EdD, UNESCO Director,
Division of Education 2030 Support
and Coordination—ED/ESC

Teaching Life provides a uniquely informed perspective on the learning needs of teachers. It is uncompromising and provocative, insisting that dominant classroom practices around 'delivering' content have to stop, alongside the reductive assessment approaches that accompany them. Quite apart from the uninspiring daily experience this leads to for teachers and learners alike, it is simply failing to provide the education that is needed in today's complex world. Professional learning is needed that supports teachers to be inquiring, critical and focused on understanding their learners as emotional, intellectual and social individuals, with important responsibilities to their fellow citizens. This needs to happen at a national scale. Armand Doucet writes with a passion born of experience of teaching and from leading brave innovations with learners and teachers. His conviction that "Teachers' voices need to be heard" in the global debates about changing education systems is impossible to ignore. Anyone setting out to develop professional learning and development for teachers should pay attention to this book. In the midst of growing concerns about the recruitment and retention of teachers, with a growing acknowledgement that teachers need opportunities to thrive, the book could not be more timely.

—Dr. Caroline Daly, Reader in Education,
UCL Institute of Education

Teaching for many of us is more than a job, more than an occupation. For those of us who have answered the call, education is at the root of our deepest passions. We love our students and love what we do. Often, the challenges we face are ignored, which only magnifies them, and this hampers student progress. Moreover, these challenges are multifaceted. Armand Doucet is an educator I look up to because he recognizes this and seeks to elevate educators, our profession, and, of course, the communities we serve. *Teaching Life* paints a well-rounded picture of teacher motivations. Doucet challenges us to remain reflective and provides suggestions as to how we might holistically impact learning and culture for the communities we love. If teaching is your calling, grab a copy, and let's collaborate.

—Estella Owoimaha-Church, Educator,
Co-founder of EN-ACT, Global Teacher
Prize Top 50 Ambassador

Doucet says the role of education is not just to prepare children for living in a more complex and technologically advanced world, but to equip them with the right level of critical thinking capability to successfully shape the world around them. It's a big challenge, but undaunted he deep dives into what makes teaching tick around the world and what it needs to do to rise to the occasion, calmly, concisely and compellingly.

—Vikas Pota, Chairman of the Varkey Foundation

Our globe is racing towards a dramatic teaching shortage, where UNESCO estimates we will be short over 69 million teachers by 2030. Doucet draws upon his own decades of work as a coach, teacher, leader, and his visits to classes across the globe to argue that education is the single most important social program for the long-term future success of any society. An award-winning teacher himself, Doucet underscores that education system must see teachers as professionals while also ensuring that education system are depoliticized. Jumping back and forth with stories from his previous career in marketing to his current classroom—Doucet highlights several flaws in the teaching profession—including inadequate time for building networks, a lack of resources for cultivating partnerships and a scarcity of thoughtful professional development. This timely and teacher-centered piece reminds us that a country that cannot think, is just as dangerous as a country that cannot defend itself.

—Maggie MacDonnell, Global Teacher
Prize Winner (2017)

Teaching Life is both a window into how teachers are currently meeting the demands of a complex, changing world and an insightful vision of how our education systems must adapt to allow our students, teachers, and society to succeed in a technological future.

—Michael Soskil, Pennsylvania Teacher of
the Year (2017–2018) and Top 10 Global
Teacher Prize Finalist (2016)

Teachers change lives and this thoughtful book shares our stories, hopes, aspirations, challenges and ability to make epic happen! I'm proud and humbled that Armand would feature the work of Green Bronx Machine and as Chief Eternal Optimist of Bronx County, I'm inspired and determined to work that much harder to grow something greater with my colleagues all around the world!

—Stephen Ritz, Top 10 Global Teacher Prize Finalist (2015) and Founder, Green Bronx Machine

A sharp view of the issues educators face in the Fourth Industrial Revolution, this book will help new and seasoned teachers go from good to great. You will be inspired and amused by the many recollections both from the authors' experience as a celebrated educator, and the stories of many exemplary teachers around the globe. This is a book for and about teachers. However it happened, we had a calling to education. We chose to embrace the teaching profession. From design thinking to technology integration to building a community and to navigating assessment, this book is both a call to action and a resource guide on how to rise above the many challenges in education today. No matter how you came into teaching, and no matter how long have you been in the classroom, you will find your voice in Doucet's words.

—Elisa Guerra, IDB's Best Educator in LatAm (2015), Global Teacher Prize Finalist (2015), Coauthor: *Teaching in the Fourth Industrial Revolution: Standing at the Precipice* **(Routledge 2018)**

Having in hand the book of Professor Doucet I can say that I found a pleasant surprise. Articulated and with a systematic view on the new realities of education, Professor Doucet demonstrates important correlations between education, knowledge and the Fourth Industrial Revolution. In a connected society (e-Earth) it becomes a sine qua non condition to understand the role that teachers occupy in this admirable 'New World.' With a very diverse life trajectory, Professor Doucet, inspires deep philosophical, technical and educational reflections in a very innovative way, relating history, project-based learning and pop culture like Harry Potter. With a unique cultural background and brilliant insight, the teacher relates from Anthony Bourdain to Pavlov with modern transformative education. I believe that people, companies and startups who wish to innovate and be in tune with society and its challenges can also benefit from reading this book. Finally, more than just a reference book, this is a guide for the new generations of teachers who wish to prepare students and citizens for the new challenges of the 21st century. I strongly recommend its reading.

—Professor Márcio de Andrade Batista, Professor, Federal University of Mato Grosso—UFMT and Top 50 Global Teacher Prize (2016, Brazil)

The book you have in your hands, written by a great educator, is full of reflections and very useful strategies. It responds to some problems that teaching poses and explores the meaning of the phenomena that affects the educational process. It brings new methodological approaches that are inserted in the reality of our time. The entire community of teachers will be deeply grateful for the methodological topicality of this book.

—Xuxo Ruiz, Top 50 Global Teacher Finalist (2018, Spain)

Doucet's authentic voice as a teacher and leader are a gift to the world. In a world where everyone has a stake in education, but so few have both a grounded understanding of its practice and a global perspective of what really matters in schools, this account offers key insights into how education needs to be shaped today and, in the decades, to come.

—Eddie Woo, Top 10 Global Teacher Prize Finalist (2018), Mister Wootube

Armand's book arrives at a time when education is at a crossroads. Teachers are standing at a junction surrounded by 'signposts' telling them to take one road over another. It is no surprise, therefore, that teachers feel like they're in a pinball machine being ricocheted from one idea to the next. Armand's book is a beacon illuminating another more optimistic and inclusive path. A path that involves different groups working together toward the common goal of creating the best education system for our children. Armand shares his story with passion and candour and in doing so provides an authentic insight into a teacher's life. I hope Armand's book encourages other teachers to share their stories as there is real power in making teaching visible. Yes, education is at a crossroads, but this is not necessarily a bad thing as it invites innovation and the chance to dream big. It also evokes hope: one of the most powerful human emotions. I thank Armand for writing a book full of hope, for out of hope comes motivation and drive. The drive to build the best education system possible for our children. Reading this book gave me hope for with voices like Armand's in educational discussions, the future looks bright.

—**Alexandra Harper, Global Teacher Prize Finalist (2015)**

In contemporary, energetic, and personally engaging language, Doucet deftly lays out education's challenges and solutions in *Teaching Life*. The book makes the case that globally, real, effective change will happen in teacher centric education. Doucet plainly states the habits of mind, empathy and technology that bring out the best in teaching. His extensive teaching experience, and global educational research underscores the purpose and direction of this important book.

—**Naomi Volain, Environmental Educator, Pasadena, CA**

There are many educators for us to learn from, but Doucet is a standout teacher-practitioner voice. In *Teaching Life*, Doucet provides a compelling narrative for readers on the *why* and *how* of redefining the role of "teacher" for the Fourth Industrial Revolution. It is a mustread for teachers: Doucet will uplift and inspire you to action in your learning environment! It's also a must-read for school leaders: Doucet will create the conditions for you to reflect on what you can do differently in your own practice to release transformation in teachers and systems. Doucet helps all readers realize it's time to honor the agency, humanity and professionalism of our teachers and change the field of education. Our learners deserve nothing less!

—**Randy Ziegenfuss, Ed.D., Superintendent of Salisbury Township School District, Allentown, PA, and Educational Podcaster**

Index

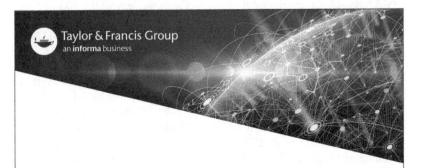